The Prince of War
Billy Graham's Crusade for a Wholly Christian Empire

Second Edition

by Cecil Bothwell

Brave Ulysses Books
2010

The Prince of War
EAN: 9781456325909
Copyright © 2007, 2010 by Cecil Bothwell
Cover design: David Lynch
Front cover photo courtesy Lyndon B. Johnson
Presidential Library
Rear cover photo by the author.
Brave Ulysses Books
POB 1877
Asheville, North Carolina 28802
braveulysses.com

also by the author
•Gorillas in the Myth: A Duck Soup Reader
2000/second edition 2008
•The Icarus Glitch: Another Duck Soup Reader
2001
•Finding Your Way in Asheville
2005/third edition 2009
**•Garden My Heart: Organic Strategies for Backyard
Sustainability**
2008
**•Pure Bunkum: Reporting on the life and crimes of
Buncombe County Sheriff Bobby Lee Medford**
2008
•Can we have archaic and idiot?
2009
**•Whale Falls: An exploratioin of belief and its
consequences**
2010

The Prince of War

to Charlie Thomas
ever an inspiration

Table of Contents

"It is when power is wedded to chronic fear that it becomes formidable."
~**Eric Hoffer**

"Christianity is the most perverted system that ever shone on man."

~**Thomas Jefferson**

Introduction

I first became curious about Billy Graham in March, 2002. Like anyone else in our culture, I had been aware of his fame, his frequent appearances with presidents and his well-attended crusades, but an Associated Press story caught my eye. It said that recently released transcripts of taped conversations in the Nixon White House included an exchange between the preacher and the President, in 1972, about the malevolent influence of Jews in the United States. As reported in newspapers across the country, the conversation appeared to have been brief, a few sentences on either side which included the suggestion from Graham that something might be done about the problem after Nixon's reelection.

Graham's public relations firm issued an apology in which the preacher disavowed his anti-Semitic comments and a rapprochement was reached with a national association of rabbis. Graham was forgiven.

Considering Nixon's reputation for meanness and paranoia, the public impression was that Graham, a polite and agreeable sort, had been pulled into a bit of unpleasantness with a close friend—something that can happen to anyone. Do we automatically knock down a buddy who tells a dumb-blonde joke, a Polish joke, an immigrant tale? We should, but do we? Not always. Graham is human too. And, after all, this wasn't just any old friend. He was the President of the United States of America. But I was curious. As an investigative reporter with, then, fifteen years of experience under my belt, I was well aware that news stories rarely contain all the facts, if for no other reason than the limitations of space. I wondered about the context of the conversation, where it began and where it ended. So I obtained the transcript.

I learned that the conversation had lasted an hour and a half, had rarely strayed from denunciation of Jews and had sometimes been led by Graham. That astonished me. Moreover, twenty minutes of conversation had been redacted before release. What, I wondered, had been suppressed?

Beyond that, I mulled Graham's career more broadly. I knew he had been more or less close to every president since Eisenhower. Later I would learn about his relationship with Truman. I knew he led prayer breakfasts and attended other official functions that splashed through the media from time to time. But what of his conversations behind closed doors? Was the Jew conversation typical or aberrational?

That was the beginning of the present volume.

The past several decades may well rank as the most fearful time in human history—given that tangible threats to human life grew far beyond ancient phantasms of myth or the unfathomable mysteries posited by ignorance. What's more, electronic media have spread bad news everywhere, live and in color, while modern print techniques erupted in the form of glossy news magazines employing photographers who fanned out across the globe.

It is no surprise that a ministry that preached fear and promised salvation could prosper in such times and Billy Graham proved expert at brandishing both stick and carrot in tents and stadia around the planet.

Graham understood early and well that a successful ministry would require professional salesmanship and he carefully cultivated contacts in the major media with an eye to presenting his work in the best possible light. At the same time, he founded his own media conglomerate of magazine, radio, television and film production which was the precursor of Focus on the Family, the 700 Club, PTL and the widely influential *Left Behind* series.

Graham's enthusiastic supporters in big media have consistently portrayed him as apolitical. As recently as February 2005, *Time* magazine reported, "He has had the ear of Presidents for five decades, but except for his public disavowal of racial segregation, Billy Graham, 86, has stuck to soul saving and left the political proselytizing to others. He explained his self-imposed separation of church and state in the language of a Gospel preacher: 'It's not what I was called to do.'"[1]

In *Time's* latest contribution to its rose-colored version of Graham's efforts, *The Preacher and the Presidents: Billy Graham in the White House* (Center Street, 2007), authors Nancy Gibbs and Michael Duffy continue in this vein. They gently poke at the preacher for his back-room political dealings, carefully skirt his advocacy for war, offer him unearned praise for leadership in civil rights and wrap it all up as a warm-and-fuzzy paean to his love and faith. Though their work contains numerous historical errors, the final sentence is spot on: "Because all along, there was really only one crusade," they conclude. The unanswered question remains. What or whom was he crusading for?

Notwithstanding his professed calling, it is apparent that Graham worked the corridors of Congress as well as the private rooms of the White House, sometimes overtly, sometimes quietly, in secret letters and private phone calls. His ministry even employed a foreign policy adviser who coordinated policy positions with occupants of the White House. And, contrary to *Time's* assertion, it seems that Graham did more to abet segregation than to end it, actively opposing Martin Luther King's use of civil disobedience while endorsing aggressive police tactics and punitive laws.

Those who scratch a presidential back are apt to have their own backs scratched a little as well, and Graham took full advantage of his access to power. Letters of introduction from chief executives opened doors for him around the world, perhaps no more so than when Ronald Reagan helped his efforts to preach behind the Iron Curtain. Graham was transported around the globe on military aircraft and not only to visit troops, though pastoral visits to Korea and Vietnam also redounded in his favor. The White House arranged donation of planes for Graham's missionary activities as well, activities that all too soon enabled genocidal disposssesion of South American native populations living in the path of oil exploration. And the CIA underwrote at least some of his crusades, albeit through front organizations of which Graham denied all knowledge.

Like many another political figure, Graham has sealed most of the personal documents connected to his life and work until after–in some cases many years after–his death. Nor did he consent to be interviewed for this work. But the published and unpublished documentary record speaks volumes. It reveals a Billy Graham who has been an unabashed nationalist and capitalist and advocate for American empire. The picture that emerges is decidedly not that of a disinterested man of the cloth. Rather, Graham often appears as a well-connected covert political operative. To the extent that this seems surprising, it stems from the public's willful naiveté concerning a self-professed holy man coupled with intentionally biased reporting from the major media at the behest of ideologues including, most prominently, William Randolph Hearst and Henry Luce.

Perhaps we should pay heed to what Graham has actually said instead of accepting his own and others' later versions of the facts. This tale is told in Graham's words and those of the biographers, historians, public figures and Presidents who knew him well.

You may be as surprised as I was at the picture that emerges in these pages. It is not the story of a man of peace.

Introduction to the Second Edition

Billy Graham has largely retreated from public view in the three years since publication of this work, though he continues to receive powerful politicos eager for his imprimatur. Presidential wannabe Sarah Palin stopped by for a photo-op and dinner in 2009. The following year President Barack Obama became the eleventh sitting U.S. president to pay his respects.

Graham's powerful media empire rolls on with Web sites, Tweets, Facebook and other social media added to radio, TV and print efforts, while his writers continue to ghost a daily advice column for newspapers around the globe.

A few passing comments in the Acknowledgments appended to this work spurred a remarkable shift in my career when I ran for elected office in Asheville, North Carolina, in 2009. Gambling interests and Sons of the Confederacy called me out for my non-theism and triggered an astonishing amount of media attention.

The story of their mail smear campaign and legal threats is told elsewhere, but my ensuing engagement with the secular community, advocates for separation of church and state, church group and university forum discussions of belief and the law, have pushed me to take much stronger and more public stands against the effort to inject religion into American government and law.

The political work Graham began in the 1950s has grown into powerful religionist lobbying organizations which succeed over and over again in bending elected officials to their bidding. We see creationism inserted into public school text books, pharmacists permitted to reject prescriptions based on faith, parochial schools permitted to use corporal punishment, faith-healing parents permitted to deny medical care to children, foreign aid dollars directed to abstinence-only efforts instead of sex education and meaningful AIDs prevention, religious hazing in the U.S. military, and much more.

The Founders well understood the dangers of state religion and the potential influence of men like Billy Graham. We must defend both freedom of- and freedom from-religion. More and more this is becoming an important part of my life's work.

— Cecil Bothwell, October 24, 2010

"We are selling the greatest product on earth.
Why shouldn't we promote it as effectively
as we promote a bar of soap?"

~Billy Graham
Saturday Evening Post, 1963

Chapter 1
The Media Man

Billy Graham was born on a prosperous 400 acre dairy farm on the outskirts of Charlotte, North Carolina, on November 7, 1918. The grandson of two former Confederate soldiers, one sworn to Ku Klux Klan membership in post-Civil War South Carolina, Graham was deeply imbued with the attitudes of the Old South and the entitlements of landed wealth. Although Graham recollects childhood years devoted to backbreaking farm labor in his autobiography, according to one of the poorly paid tenant workers it was his brother, Melvin, who put in long hours. "Billy didn't believe in work," the former employee recalled.[2]

Melvin had similar memories. "He was quick at that milking all right—he could milk a cow in about four minutes, where it takes most people about ten minutes. That was just how much he didn't like doing it."[3] His brother is being generous in his description because anyone who has milked a cow knows that any shortcut is a failing that is uncomfortable for the cow and bad for the farm.

The farm had been left to Franklin Graham and his younger brother, Clyde, while their eldest sibling, Thomas, went off to Oklahoma to make a fortune in oil, cattle and cotton gins. Uncle Tom's wealth made a lasting impression on young Billy who described Thomas on his return home each summer, "He had gone out there and married this Cherokee Indian and made a fortune in cattle and cotton and oil, and he came back home in the biggest automobile any of us had ever seen."[4]

Frank had a reputation as a sharp operator and Clyde's wife, fearing her husband's eventual exclusion from the family wealth, pressed for legal partition to secure their rights. Frank continued the dairy business on his 300 acre share and made a fortune selling off land for commercial development as the city of Charlotte gradually expanded. At one point he convinced the municipality to run a water line to his home (then located outside city limits) and promptly turned around to collect one hundred dollar hookup fees from neighbors along the pipeline. On another occasion he and his lawyer met with the city council in closed session where he tearfully explained his need for a variance to gain some small benefit from his property. Soon an IBM office building rose on the site of the family homestead, together with Charlotte's first modern shopping center.

A former neighbor reported, "Frank Graham was always just a little too sharp in his business dealings. Like when he heard that Esso was thinking about putting up an office building on the property he co-owned with Guy Carswell. What he did was quickly buy out Carswell, without ever mentioning that particular little bit of information that he had happened on."[5]

Along the way, Frank Graham availed himself of cheap labor from German prisoners held in Charlotte during World War II. One former farmhand said, "He went down there one morning and worked some kinda deal, and we started to bring a load of 'em up every morning and taking 'em back every night, working 'em hauling hay and gathering corn and pickling beans. ... He used 'em on must of been several months. Nosirree, he didn't let much get by him."[6]

Billy was the first of four siblings. Next came a sister, Catherine, then Melvin the hard worker who was five years Billy's junior and, finally, another sister, Jean.

During an unremarkable high school career Billy spent every night for two months attending one of holy roller Mordecai Ham's crusades and announced his "decision for Christ." His decision may have been helped along by the many Sunday afternoons he had spent listening to his apocalyptic Uncle Simon rant and rail about the glories of the Second Coming. During the balance of Ham's Charlotte revival Graham urged classroom peers to join his nightly forays to the big tent.

Ham was a great admirer of the pro-fascist Henry Ford and laced his sermons with quotes from the automaker and the spurious *Protocols of the Elders of Zion*. Graham biographer

Marshall Frady notes that Ham "was one of his era's most gaudy and livid anti-Semites., fulminating against 'apostate Jewry' and 'the wicked Jews who killed Jesus." These are the same accusations that would tumble to tape from Graham's lips years later in the Nixon Oval Office. "The Bible says there are satanic Jews, and that's where our problem arises," he told Nixon.

Whereas he had previously enjoyed a reputation among schoolmates and teachers as a tattletale who frequently provoked trouble while avoiding consequences himself, he now became a self-righteous scold. A mechanic repairing a flat tire on Graham's car banged his thumb and muttered, "Christ!" The young Graham told him off and he responded, "This is a free country, sonny. I can do what I damn well please and say what I damn well please."

Graham shot back, "Not around me, you can't!" and the offended mechanic raised a tire iron threateningly. The boy trumped his opponent with a monetary threat, "I'll tell my daddy if you do that. My daddy's Mr. Frank Graham, and he brings all his Deere trucks in here."[7]

Nor had he left behind his hereditary biases. A friend from his youth recalled recommending "a colored barbershop ... where they give great haircuts, real cheap," and Billy's reply: "Long as there's a white barbershop in Charlotte, I'll never have my hair cut at a nigger barbershop. Never."[8]

His father, Franklin, employed numerous black and Hispanic farm laborers while his mother, Morrow, had the help of a black cook. In turn, his son, William Franklin Graham III, has said he proudly displays a Confederate flag bumper sticker on his pick-up truck.

When Billy and Ruth set up housekeeping in Montreat, they too would employ a succession of "yard-men" and a full time black cook. Though he is credited with integrating his crusades, at least following the Supreme Court decision in Brown v. Board of Education, Graham would prove slow to do so in his personal life as would be revealed by his active membership in an exclusionary country club as late as the 1990s.

After high school, at the urging of a fellow Christian convert, he became a Fuller Brush Company sales representative. Graham quickly learned the art of inserting a foot into an open door, proffering free merchandise and clinching deals with the unwilling, but because Graham was given to selling Christianity as well as boar and horse bristles, his supervisor had to field repeated complaints from customers who wanted scrub brushes without the sermon. Though his job began and ended with sales, years later he bragged that he had lied to prospective customers. "My approach was to say to the housewife, 'Well, I haven't come here to sell you anything, I've come to give you a brush."[9] Soon he was the most successful peddler in North or South Carolina.

In 1936 Graham headed off for a brief stint at Bob Jones College, an unaccredited Bible school in Cleveland, Tennessee. However, the grim drudgery at Bob Jones quickly paled, particularly when he heard from a friend that circumstances were less austere at the Florida Bible Institute, a tiny college operating on the grounds of a former resort hotel. A midwinter visit impressed him with balmy weather, fresh oranges and surrounding lakes and he applied for admission. When the school demurred, Graham's mother successfully intervened, writing the school's president to explain that Tennessee's climate was too harsh for her boy who had been claiming to suffer from flu-like symptoms for months. He later acknowledged to a biographer that it was "mostly a case of miserableness," but that, "I told my parents it was the flu."[10]

Financial inducements may have been a factor as well since many students at the tiny Florida school were on a work-fare program, whereas Graham arrived with full parental support. "My father was paying my expenses and providing my pocket money," he later wrote in his autobiography, *Just As I Am.* "So I was affluent compared to some of the other students."[11] Graham arrived at the school in his father's brand new convertible and soon acquired his own car, a 1929 Chevy coupe. Soon he was preaching at local churches and revivals, and declared that God had laid the heavy burden on him of seeking ordination as a minister.

Talk show host Larry King spoke to Graham about that experience in June, 2005, and asked, "You had an experience once standing on a hill, right? A long time ago? How did you find

God the first time?" In response, Graham spoke of his Associate Reformed Presbyterian upbringing and his high school evangelical conversion and added, "[L]ater, on a golf course in Florida, I felt called to preach the gospel. And one night in the full moon and the palm trees around where our school was, I knelt down there alone. And I said, 'Lord, I'll do what you want me to do and go where you want me to go,' and that was another big spiritual experience for me."[12]

He took up golf as well, and would rack up an impressive roster of foursomes over the years including numerous U.S. Presidents, Hollywood stars, industrial magnates and foreign heads of state.

In 1940 Graham transferred to Wheaton College, deemed by some to be the Harvard of evangelistic training. His matriculation began on the same golf course, caddying for two wealthy Chicago businessmen who took a shine to Graham and offered to subsidize a year's room, board and tuition at their local seminary. School authorities in the suburban Chicago college examined his year at Bob Jones and three year tenure in Florida and gave him credit for only one year's work. On the advice of a friend he opted to major in anthropology, "because it was the study of man, and also it was easy."[13] He soon met and began dating Ruth McCue Bell, daughter of one of the most powerful men in the Christian missionary world, Dr. L. Nelson Bell, a surgeon from Virginia who had settled in Asheville, North Carolina. Bell, also active in politics, would prove enormously helpful to Graham's career through his contacts, financial support and mentoring.

Dr. John P. Holt, an Asheville native and second-generation physician as well as school board member, was acquainted with Bell. "Nelson Bell lived one block from our house on College Street," Holt recalled. "I can remember walking right by where he lived almost daily. He was a tall, good-looking man and the leader of the John Birch Society in town. At the time, the Birch Society was very prominent because the anti-civil rights attitude was beginning to develop. and John Birch was the most anti-civil rights organization in Asheville."

The John Birch Society was vehemently anti-communist and pro-libertarian. It strenuously defended the purportedly Judeo-Christian bent of the U.S. Constitution and idealized the Founding Fathers as anti-communists. The society embraced a conspiracy-theory view of history and labeled Eisenhower a possible "conscious, dedicated agent of the Communist Conspiracy." During the 1960s, The John Birch Society opposed the Civil Rights Movement generally, alleging communist influence, and the 1964 Civil Rights Act, asserting that it was in violation of the Tenth Amendment—the reservation of otherwise unspecified powers to the states or to the people. There were close ties to the Ku Klux Klan and across the South it was often accepted wisdom that the JBS was the public face of the more secretive KKK, though members heatedly denied the connection when confronted.

After their graduation in 1943, the couple married in the Bell's adopted home of Montreat, not far from Asheville, and returned to Chicago. There Graham embarked on his first pastorate in Western Springs, a village some twenty-five miles from the city, and initiated his first radio ministry. Meanwhile, he founded a Professional Men's Club downtown and began his lifelong cultivation of well-heeled businessmen. While his rural church had only thirty-five parishioners, the urban club soon drew crowds of three hundred doctors, lawyers and politicos to its monthly meetings.

With World War II in full throat, Graham elected to join the military as a chaplain, an obligation forestalled by the army's requirement that he first complete a year as a practicing minister. At the end of the requisite year he was commissioned as a second lieutenant and was due to enter a chaplain's training course at Harvard Divinity School when he informed authorities that he was too ill to travel, immediately obtained a discharge and went to Florida to convalesce—living on a stipend provided by a concerned radio listener. Fellow evangelist Charles Templeton had joined him in Florida and quickly convinced Graham to enlist in a new venture called Youth for Christ. Templeton was a Canadian cartoonist turned self-educated evangelist and Christian broadcaster who would later declare himself an agnostic, move on to Princeton Seminary and be drummed out of evangelical circles.

Graham resigned as pastor in Western Springs and appointed himself the first full-time paid employee of Youth for Christ while Chicago pastor Torrey Johnson (sometimes also credited as founder of YFC) was president of the organization. Johnson would later tour Europe as a YFC evangelist.

Youth for Christ's techniques were published in 1944 by Johnson and Bob Cook (later president of the National Religious Broadcasters). Their four keys for successful evangelistic rallies were: radio coverage; an entertaining program; slick promotion; and preaching laced with mentions of current events. Graham quickly adopted those methods as his own. The early YFC rallies included Bible quiz shows, magic acts, ventriloquists, barbershop quartets and a counting horse able to tap twelve times when queried about the number of Christ's disciples. That same year he launched his first local radio ministry on Chicago's WCFL radio.

Graham's lifelong travels began in earnest and Ruth moved back to Montreat to live with her parents. The evangelist logged 200,000 miles in the first year of his youth ministry, with occasional layovers in Montreat where Ruth gave birth to five children between 1945 and 1958. Graham received word of the births by word of mouth or telegram and when the fourth child, Franklin, was old enough to talk, his reaction to one of his father's infrequent arrivals was, "Who's him?"[14]

In sermonizing about marriage and a woman's role, Graham would quote the Bible. "As a result of sin, God cursed the woman, and the fact that she has suffered in childbirth is a result of the fall, that first sin of her disobedience. God said, 'In sorrow shalt thou bring forth children, and thy desire shall be to thy husband, and he shall rule over thee.'"[15] There is no evidence that either Graham saw reason to deviate from that injunction.

During his first Asheville crusade, Graham held separate events for men and women, in order to provide them with separate messages about marriage. According to press coverage, "Graham belabored men for unfaithfulness to their wives and said they were bringing 'wreck, raid and ruin' to their homes by immorality." Then he "Thrashed the women verbally for ignoring habits of cleanliness and beauty care. He scanned the thousands of women and advised, 'some of you could use a little make-up.' He tucked his arm snugly, as though in that of the Lord's, and demanded: 'How would you dress if Jesus were your escort tonight?'"

He went on to blame schooling for the breakdown of the American family. "We thought that education would bring about happy homes but we have more misery and unhappiness in the home today than any time in the history of the United States." He also claimed, "Most of the juvenile delinquency in America today can be traced to broken homes." Apparently he cited no source for this assertion that well-educated, divorced parents were spawning criminals, and then repeated his standard recipe for marital contentment. "God does teach a governmental arrangement of the family in which he places the husband at the head. The wives are to fit into the mold of the husband." He quoted Genesis 3:16 concerning husband-rule and said, "Wives are to submit to their husbands: they are to be in subjection to them, obedient to them and to love them. If you fail in any of these the Word of God can be blasphemed and you will have your prayers hindered."16

Even sixty-four years later, after a stream of books and articles which depicted their union as mutually supportive and happy, after tearful declarations of his deep love for Ruth, Billy would elect to countermand her publicly stated and frequently repeated burial wishes after she slipped into what would prove to be a terminal coma. Ruth's prayers, at least, seem to have gone unanswered.

Concurrent with Graham's career launch, the Wisconsin Republican Senate primary of 1946 marked the rise of Joe McCarthy to national prominence. His campaign rhetoric concerning an alleged communist conspiracy would grow into what was later known as the Red Scare of the 1950s. Senator McCarthy's distortions and outright lies threatened civil liberties and destroyed careers. Graham would become one of his most loyal and enduring allies.

Then, in 1947, unrelenting temperance advocate and anti-evolutionist William Bell Riley, sometimes credited as inventor of the label "fundamentalist," and founder of Northwestern Schools in Minneapolis, recruited Graham to succeed him as president of his school. Three years' tenure in that position and growing fame on the tent-meeting circuit led to Graham's founding of the Billy Graham Evangelistic Association in 1950. Initially staffed with Northwestern alumni, BGEA was headquartered in Minnesota until son Franklin Graham assumed the helm and moved operations to Charlotte in 2005.

Graham's official biographers generally credit his powerful sermonizing, energy, good looks and a dollop of divine providence for his success, but a great deal of credit is due his early grasp of the power of mass media. Like Bing Crosby, who propelled himself to fame through early adoption of recording technology, or Elvis Presley, the first heavily-promoted white performer to popularize black music on the cusp of new solid-state transistor technology, Graham and a circle of astute collaborators made it their business to dominate media evangelism. He wasn't the first preacher on the radio, but he quickly moved to prominence via his nationally broadcast Hour of Decision (1950 to present).

In 1949 he rejected film offers from Hollywood but formed his own film company two years later, naming himself CEO of World Wide Pictures. The company churned out evangelically inspired films which were translated into multiple languages. Graham later bragged that a World Wide film was showing somewhere on earth every hour of every day all year round.

Beginning in 1957 Graham engineered nationwide, later worldwide, telecasts of his crusades and, in 1962, founded a radio station, WFGW/WMIT, in Black Mountain, North Carolina, which soon developed a global, multi-lingual reach. Nor did he neglect the medium of print, starting with a daily advice column, "My Answer" (1952 to present), and then magazine publishing, *Christianity Today* (1956 to present) and *Decision* (1960 to present).

While Graham traveled many miles in those early years he first came to national prominence in October, 1949, in the course of a multi-week tent revival in Los Angeles. True to his media game plan, organizers spent $25,000 on advertising the event, the equivalent of $215,000 in 2007 dollars according to the

Consumer Price Index. His rapid rise to fame was fashioned by two publishing titans, William Randolph Hearst and Henry Luce, who saw in Graham the perfect spokesperson for the anticommunist message they urgently wanted to convey.

Graham's Los Angeles appearance caught Hearst's attention, stirring a perfect storm of media influence, politics and religion that would accelerate the minister's rise to stardom. As reported by Ben Bagdikian in his seminal work, *The Media Monopoly,* "Hearst and Luce interviewed the obscure preacher and decided he was worthy of their support. Billy Graham became an almost instantaneous national and, later, international figure preaching anti communism. In late 1949 Hearst sent a telegram to all Hearst editors: 'Puff Graham.' The editors did—in Hearst newspapers, magazines, movies and newsreels. Within two months Graham was preaching to crowds of 350,000."[17]

In another version of the story, reported by Doug Reed in 1953, "Then, aging William Randolph Hearst, from his San Fernando Valley ranch, heard of Billy and called him to his house. Conversations followed and friendship was met. Hearst, convinced of Billy's sincerity and popular appeal, gave the word. And all down the long Hearst chain of newspapers went the word: 'Boost Billy Graham. Front-page Billy Graham.' Obedient editors responded and other papers followed. National magazines followed suit including *Time, Life* and *Look,* then a flood of others."[18]

Hearst's publicity push and the consequent boost in rally attendance led directly to incorporation of BGEA when Graham's cohort found itself in possession of a cardboard box crammed with cash donations totaling $25,000 during his 1950 Portland, Oregon, crusade. The bank informed the ministry that the IRS wouldn't consider the deposit to be tax-free without the required nonprofit paperwork and a representative rushed out from Minneapolis to collect signatures from Billy, Ruth and others in the entourage.

In just five years, Graham and company had leveraged his ministry from a suburban Chicago bywater to the national stage.

"Billy Graham represents a basic kind of patriotism in this country—an unquestioning, obeying patriotism, a loyalty to the authority of the president. Billy was always uncritical, unchallenging, unquestioning."

~Bill Moyers
quoted by Robert Sherrill
"Preachers to Power"
The Nation, July 13, 1998

Chapter 2
First Shots

The latter half of the twentieth century was dominated by a war that could be called "cold" only if viewed through a weirdly skewed lens. Millions died in conventional and guerrilla battles while the unending fight was overhung by that looming threat of nuclear annihilation. The same confrontation is no longer called cold, having morphed into an apparently permanent assault on an enemy labeled terror—an effort which observers ranging from Chalmers Johnson to Kevin Phillips to Zbigniew Brzezinski have suggested may undo the United States through over-extension if not bankruptcy—while the threat of nuclear undoing continues to grow. Today's children are spared the inanity of duck-and-cover drills, even as they inherit the pervasive dread that it could all end tomorrow, whether by weapon or disease.

Children of the mid-twentieth century learned what two small atomic bombs had done to Hiroshima and Nagasaki. There were pictures, reports and interviews with survivors. The arsenals had grown far more horrific in the post war years. Nervous fingers were poised beside buttons that could make the sky fall and the oceans evaporate.

"Within weeks of the destruction of Hiroshima and Nagasaki ... all the familiar signs of nuclear fear were already in place—newspapers were drawing concentric circles of atomic destruction outward from fantasy Ground Zeroes in American cities, and magazines were offering visions of our country as a vaporized wasteland, while imagining millions of Americans dead."[19]

Each newsreel of mushroom clouds billowing up over Pacific atolls and every multipage spread in *Life* magazine depicting the power of the atom made death seem nearer the door. A new kind of existential dread seemed to pervade America and the focus of that fear was quickly directed toward the Soviet Union.

Though Graham had crisscrossed the country for several years and, according to biographer John Pollock, "had a growing reputation in North America as an evangelist for 'city-wide campaigns',"[20] the final day of the Los Angeles event, with a push from Hearst, overflowed the nine thousand seats available and was reportedly the largest such gathering since Billy Sunday's New York campaign in 1917.

During the Los Angeles revival, President Truman's announcement that the Russians had successfully tested an atomic bomb and were building a nuclear arsenal stunned the nation. Graham immediately ramped up the anti-communist message in his sermons, preaching that, "Western culture and its fruits had its foundation in the Bible, the Word of God, and in the revivals of the the Seventeenth and Eighteenth Centuries. Communism, on the other hand, has decided against God, against Christ, against the Bible, and against all religion. Communism is not only an economic interpretation of life -- communism is a religion that is inspired, directed, and motivated by the Devil himself who has declared war against Almighty God."[21]

Graham didn't hesitate to invent facts to bolster his message. "Do you know the area that is marked out for the enemy's first atomic bomb? New York! Secondly, Chicago; and thirdly, the city of Los Angeles."[22] The Soviets had just set off their first device and, somehow, Graham already had inside information on their targeting strategy. Henceforth, cataclysmic war would take its place alongside hell and damnation as frequent themes in Graham's sermons.

The anti-communist message (communism is "more rampant in Los Angeles than in any other city in America."[23]) resonated with Hearst, a rabid anti-communist who had voiced support for Hitler and the German Nazis in the lead-up to World War II. Hearst issued the two-word command, "Puff Graham," to his editors across the country and privately "puffed" Graham himself, to Wall Street magnate Bernard Baruch.

Graham's anti-communist drumbeat was entirely consonant with that of President Harry S. Truman, who ignored Japan's pleas for peace in order to demonstrate the efficacy of this country's atomic weapons to Josef Stalin. That the war was over before Hiroshima and Nagasaki were laid waste is no longer questioned by mainstream historians. The terms for peace requested by Japan before the Bomb was dropped were the same terms accepted by Truman in its aftermath.

Following World War II, a war-weary American populace was happy to downsize the military and return to peacetime pursuits. But Truman, and perhaps more importantly, Allen Dulles and Dean Acheson, carefully cultivated unreasoning fear in the American public to justify rearmament and the vast expenditures for weaponry that such a policy would entail.

Dulles (soon to become the longest enduring head of the CIA) and Acheson (Truman's Secretary of State and later an advisor to Presidents Kennedy, Johnson and Nixon), worked to demonize the Soviet Union and Communism in order to put the United States on the permanent wartime footing it has henceforth maintained. As this country unilaterally abrogated treaties signed with the Soviet Union, that nation was cast as an evil empire (though the specific phrase would await use until the "great communicator" Ronald Reagan took his turn as President). Thus were U.S. citizens herded into support for militarization and relentless military intervention around the globe.

The Federation of American Scientists has documented that this country engaged in close to two hundred wars or interventions between 1946 and 2006, none of them declared and all of them justified by the alleged threats of communism or terrorism.

Fear of God, death or hell is the stock-in-trade of evangelists, comprising the necessary setup before the pitch. William Martin offered an explanation in his 1991 account of Graham's early sermons, "... even those whose personal lives seemed rich and fulfilling must live in a world filled with terror and threat. As a direct result of sinful humanity's rebellion against God, our streets have become jungles of terror, mugging, rape, and death. Confusion reigns on campuses as never before. Political leaders live in constant fear of the assassin's bullet. Racial tension seems certain to unleash titanic forces of hatred and violence. Communism threatens to eradicate freedom from the face of the earth. Small nations are getting the bomb, so that global war seems inevitable. High-speed objects, apparently guided by an unknown intelligence, are coming into our atmosphere for reasons no one understands. Clearly, all signs point to the end of the present world order. ...

"Graham's basic mode of preaching in these early years was assault. ... Then, when he had his listeners mentally crouching in terror, aware that all the attractively labeled escape routes—alcohol, sexual indulgence, riches, psychiatry, education, social-welfare programs, increased military might, the United Nations—led ultimately to dead ends, he held out the only compass that pointed reliably to the straight and narrow path that leads to personal happiness and lasting peace."[24]

Graham's message of fear also resonated with a then more famous fearmonger, South Carolina's racist Governor Strom Thurmond. Graham was staying in the governor's mansion during a 1950 crusade in Columbia when Baruch convinced Luce to pay him a visit. Luce and Graham hit it off immediately and the largest national news magazines were soon added to the Hearst papers as "puffers" of the ministry.

As noted by reporter and biographer Neal Thompson, "Henry Luce believed that the psychological battleground of the cold war was no place for anti-American stories, a belief reflected in the semi-propagandistic stories of not only *Life* magazine but other publications in his empire."[25] Having published nearly 600 stories involving Graham since 1950, Luce's *Time* magazine probably contributed more to the preacher's global fame than any other news source. In recent years the magazine has continued its founder's legacy, prominently featuring Graham's son Franklin and his late-blooming evangelical career as heir to the ministry, and capping its fauning coverage with the release of *The Preacher and the Presidents* in 2007.

Life magazine lauded Graham soon after the pivotal Luce interview, reporting in March, 1950, "Billy Graham, a thirty-one-year-old evangelist who rose to prominence barely six months ago in Los Angeles was staging a spellbinding revival campaign in Columbia, South Carolina. ... Before the meeting was over 2,000 persons had swarmed out of the 'stands and knelt before Graham ..."[26]

The following month, Graham took his crusade to Boston Common while Truman threatened war with Russia. Graham called for the President and Congress to declare a national day of repentance and offered a five point peace program which included, "We must maintain strong military power for defense at any cost," and "We must strengthen organizations like the FBI for internal protection."[27]

As reported in *The Boston Daily Globe,* "Emphasizing his first point in the plan for peace, Graham said, 'We must prepare for war even while we are at peace. We are concerned about the cutback in defense budgets. We must get ready for anything that may happen.'"[28]

Defense spending had been sharply reduced after the conclusion of World War II, and the armed forces substantially demobilized. The U.S. was at peace despite Truman's saber rattling toward the new member of the nuclear club, and North Korea's surprise (some would say, "provoked") attack on its southern neighbor was still two months away.

"Let me tell you that the international situation is far worse than most Americans realize," Graham warned. Then, laying claim to the sort of insider information that would become a hallmark of his international policy pronouncements, he declaimed, "A few hours ago a very well-informed man told me that the President has flown back from Florida for a conference with defense leaders." Playing the fear card again, he went on, "Millions of little people throughout the world are afraid of war. They tremble as they look into the future." Then came his apocalyptic warning, "Time is drawing to a close."[29]

As late as June 20, 1950, U.S. Secretary of State Dean Acheson would tell Congress that no war was likely on the Korean peninsula. Graham's rhetoric, putatively directed toward peace, actually fanned the flames of militarism. With Graham's help, Truman, Acheson and Dulles worked their magic on Congress and the populace, and began a military buildup that lasts to the present day.

One of the many generous biographies published by the Billy Graham Evangelistic Association, *Billy Graham: God's Ambassador,* states, "Every U.S. President since World War II has found occasion and reason to call on Billy, who readily responded."[30] Historians, presidential secretaries and the Presidents themselves have described the relationship somewhat differently, with Graham the constant supplicant seeking Presidential attention. All of the chief executives save Jimmy Carter were nevertheless eager to avail themselves of Graham's influence with evangelical voters. Nor was Graham ever shy about working both sides of a contest. After Truman defeated Republican presidential candidate Governor Thomas E. Dewey in the 1948 race, Graham hired Dewey as his personal lawyer.

Several months after winning Luce's support, the newly famous minister was angling for his first White House audience, enlisting congressmen from North and South Carolina who pressed a Massachusetts congressman close to Harry Truman to make the connection. After initial rejection, he was finally scheduled for an audience on July 14, 1950.

On June 25, North Korean troops invaded South Korea and Graham sent Truman a telegram:

"MILLIONS OF CHRISTIANS PRAYING GOD GIVE YOU WISDOM IN THIS CRISIS. STRONGLY URGE SHOWDOWN WITH COMMUNISM NOW. MORE CHRISTIANS IN SOUTHERN KOREA PER CAPITA THAN ANY PART OF WORLD. WE CANNOT LET THEM DOWN."[31]

It was the first time Billy Graham urged a president to go to war. It would not be the last. Nor was the information contained in the telegram anywhere close to accurate. According to multiple historical sources, Korea's Christian population has grown rapidly in recent years, to perhaps twenty-eight percent of the total as of 2005. In 1950 the self-described Christian population of the U.S. was above eighty percent, with similarly high percentages of devotees in Canada, Mexico, most European and South American countries as well as Australia and New Zealand. Graham's assertion was completely groundless.

As related in Graham's autobiography, *Just As I Am*, his first presidential audience was less than stellar. After describing the success of his recent revivals and reaffirming his support for Truman's fledgling war effort, Graham questioned and admonished the president, a fellow Baptist, for his shortcomings in matters of faith. He then pressed the diffident president into a prayer to close the meeting. He put his arm around Truman and prayed aloud for five minutes, echoed by "Amen!" and "Do it Lord!" from his entourage.

Exiting the White House, Graham and company reenacted the visit and recounted the entire interaction to an eager Washington press corps. Truman was furious at the kiss-and-tell preacher, and Graham was never invited back. Memos pulled from the files of the Billy Graham Center at Wheaton College record an active effort by Truman to avoid all future contact. On Dec. 4, 1951, anticipating Graham's D.C. crusade in January, Secretary to the President William D. Hassett issued a directive to Matthew J. Connelly, (also Secretary to the President): "When, as and if a request comes for Billy Graham to be received at the White House, the President requests that it be turned down because of the extraordinary pressure of official business during January and February."[32]

On Dec. 28, a second memorandum to Connelly read, "At Key West the President said very decisively that he did not wish to endorse Billy Graham's Washington revival meeting and particularly he said he did not want to receive him at the White House. You remember what a show of himself Billy Graham made the last time he was here. The President does not want it repeated." [33]

Later, Truman would say, "Graham has gone off the beam. He's ... well, I hadn't ought to say this, but he's one of those counterfeits I was telling you about. He claims he's a friend of all the presidents, but he was never a friend of mine when I was president. I just don't go for people like that. All he's interested in is getting his name in the paper."[34]

Almost as soon as Truman opted for war, Graham began to criticize him for the way in which America had entered Korea and for what he believed was a lack of resolve in its execution. He asked his audiences, "How many of you voted to go into the Korean War? I never did."[35] Graham particularly faulted

Truman for not taking allied commander General Douglas MacArthur's advice to expand the war into China.

Truman's firing of MacArthur for insubordination played badly with the public and the President's popularity nose-dived. As related by David Halberstam in his last-published essay, "In time, MacArthur made an all-out frontal challenge to Truman, criticizing him to the press, almost daring the president to get rid of him. Knowing that the general had title to the flag and to the emotions of the country, while he himself merely had title to the Constitution, Truman nonetheless fired him. It was a grave constitutional crisis—nothing less than the concept of civilian control of the military was at stake. If there was irony to this, it was that MacArthur and his journalistic boosters, such as *Time* magazine owner Henry Luce, always saw Truman as the little man and MacArthur as the big man."[36] Graham happily embraced popular sentiment and blasted Truman's action publicly as he began a backstage campaign for Dwight David Eisenhower.

Notwithstanding Truman's unfriendly reception Graham continued to send unsolicited advice via telegram. In a Western Union missive dated Dec 24, 1951, the minister suggested:

"LET'S RAISE MONEY TO FREE OUR FLYERS HELD CAPTIVE BY PUBLIC SUBSCRIPTION. IT WOULD DO MORE THAN ANYTHING I KNOW TO IMPRESS THE SERIOUSNESS OF THE PRESENT CRISIS ON THE AMERICAN PEOPLE. IT WOULD HELP UNITE US BEHIND THE DEFENSE PROGRAM."[37]

Also in 1951, exhibiting what would emerge as lifelong advocacy for militarism, he told the *Charlotte Observer,* "We must maintain the strongest military establishment on earth."[38] At home, in the North Carolina mountains, Graham's personal fear demanded that he sleep with a loaded gun beside the bed. His prescription for the country was different only in scale.

"Religion and science both profess peace (and the sincerity of the professors is not being doubted), but each always turns out to have a dominant part in any war that is going or contemplated."

~Howard Nemerov
U.S. Poet Laureate

Chapter 3
Saluting a General

Early in 1952, Graham had decided to stage a Washington revival with its final rally on the steps of the Capitol. Told that this would not be permitted, he called Sid Richardson, a Texas oil billionaire and one of the richest men in the world, who had been recruited as a financial backer during the 1951 Fort Worth crusade. Richardson was a key supporter of House Speaker Sam Rayburn. Rayburn pushed through an act of Congress permitting Graham to hold the first religious service ever conducted on the Capitol steps as well as daily prayer services at the Pentagon during his crusade, another first.

From the Capitol steps he sounded a theme that would echo throughout his career, "We must maintain strong military power for defense at any cost."[39] During that crusade, Graham announced he wanted to interview every potential candidate for the presidency—though he insisted he would not publicly take sides in the coming election. By all appearances, however, he had already made up his mind in 1951 when he wrote Richardson, "The American people have come to the point where they want a man with honesty, integrity, and spiritual power. I believe the General has it."[40] Richardson passed the letter along to General Dwight D. ("Ike") Eisenhower who wrote back to Graham in the fall of 1951 reiterating his oft-repeated public demurral. He wasn't interested in running for office. Graham replied that he was praying that God would "guide you in the greatest decision of your life. Upon this decision could well rest the destiny of the Western World."[41]

Shortly after the Washington crusade, Graham and his entourage headed for Europe. On his first day in Paris, in March, he was warmly received by Eisenhower at his headquarters. How much influence the young preacher who claimed 16 million followers in the United States might have had on the reluctant general is anybody's guess. But there is no question that Ike liked

Billy, or at least what Billy represented. This was to be the beginning of an alliance that would last until Eisenhower's death in 1969.

As described by Eisenhower biographer and Professor of Religious Studies Ira Chernus, "Like his Christian forbears, Ike believed that people are naturally selfish. If they are going to live together, their desires must be restrained. Freedom, he once said, is merely 'the opportunity for self-discipline.' The only alternative he could see was to have the government impose restraints from above. He fought communism because he feared it would deprive people of their freedom to control themselves. But he saw the communists as only one in an endless procession of groups and movements threatening freedom. Freedom would always have enemies."[42] The fit with Graham's thinking could hardly have been more comfortable.

While Graham urged Ike to run, he differed sharply with Eisenhower concerning Truman's firing of MacArthur. Ignoring the advice of most U.S. military commanders, including Eisenhower and the Joint Chiefs of Staff, MacArthur had staged a daring and successful invasion of North Korea. China had responded by sending 200,000 soldiers across the Yalu River into North Korea, dividing the United Nations forces under MacArthur's command. Convinced of his own brilliance, the General decided that the best way to deal with China's full scale entry into the war was to bomb bridges across the Yalu and institute a full sea blockade to be followed by an invasion by Chiang Kai Shek's (Nationalist) army, based in Formosa.

Eisenhower, then Supreme Commander of the North Atlantic Treaty Organization, opposed the plan, and General Omar Bradley, expressing the viewpoint of the Joint Chiefs, told Congress, it was "the wrong war, at the wrong place and at the wrong time, and with the wrong enemy."

MacArthur insisted and released his plan to the press on March 24, 1951, flouting Truman's specific directive to make no public pronouncement on policy without Presidential permission. The General followed with a letter to Congressman Joseph Martin, the Republican minority leader in the House, which Martin, who supported the invasion, promptly released as well. After consultation with the Joint Chiefs and his cabinet, Truman fired MacArthur.

There were calls for impeachment of the President and McCarthy denounced Truman as "a s.o.b. who decided to remove MacArthur when drunk."[43] A Gallup poll found Americans favoring MacArthur versus Truman by 69 to 29 percent. Graham enthusiastically concurred, favorably comparing MacArthur to George Washington and declaring, "He is one of the greatest Americans of all time!"[44]

In so doing, Graham helped feed a groundswell of negative public opinion concerning Truman. While the President and the United Nations had successfully conducted a limited war, turning back the invasion and beginning armistice negotiations just thirteen months from its inception, most Republicans and some members of Great Britain's Labour Party painted it as a miserable failure. The Republican campaign in 1952 emphasized the Democrats' "betrayal" of Chiang Kai-shek in China , "loss" of the Korean War and alleged failure of Truman's effort to contain the Soviets in Europe

Once Eisenhower was nominated, Graham visited him in Denver and gave him a signed red-bound Bible which the General would keep on his bedside table for years. (It was Graham's custom to distribute autographed silk-sewn red Moroccan leather bibles to crusade workers and friends.) The evangelist laced his sermons with pro-Republican comments throughout the campaign and on the eve of the election announced the results of what he described as a personal survey of "nearly two hundred churchmen and religious editors from thirty states and twenty-two denominations."[45] Seventy-seven percent, he asserted, favored Eisenhower.

He told the press, "The Christian people of America will not sit idly by during the 1952 presidential campaign. [They] are going to vote as a bloc for the man with the strongest moral and spiritual platform, regardless of his views on other matters."[46]

Immediately following the parties' nominating conventions, both held in Chicago that year, Graham's organization played it's customary fear card. Posters for Youth For Christ rallies in the Windy City asked, "ARE WE ELECTING OUR LAST PRESIDENT?" During the ensuing presidential election campaign, despite protestations of neutrality, Graham preached a conservative Republican line. He blasted the Truman administration for failure to declare war in Korea and spoke of a lack of resolve in pursuit of victory.

Following Eisenhower's victory in November, Graham paid a brief Christmas visit to troops in Korea and returned claiming to have his own plan for victory there which he intended to share with the president-elect. "His plan was a national day of prayer for God's help in finding the precise solution to the war. Eisenhower's solution was to rely on secular military expertise; the war continued for sixteen more months."[47] Though peace talks were ongoing at the time and fighting was greatly reduced, the refusal of U.N. held prisoners of war to return to North Korea remained a major stumbling block and no armistice was ever signed.

Eisenhower became the first president to lead a prayer as part of his own inauguration, written in consultation with Graham, and shortly afterward he was baptized in the White House. Following the new President's first speech on foreign policy, Graham publicly compared the talk to the Sermon on the Mount.

McCarthy continued to spread lies and innuendo about a communist conspiracy that reached all the way to the White House. As early as 1950 a Senate committee had reported that McCarthy's charges were "a fraud and a hoax perpetrated on the Senate of the United States and on the American people. They represent perhaps the most nefarious campaign of half-truth and untruth in the history of the Republic." Notwithstanding those findings, McCarthy increased his attacks and gained a nationwide following.

Ultimately, following full investigation or trial, not one of the hundreds of accused "subversives" in the state department was ever found guilty but the atmosphere was poisonous. Truman declined to run for reelection.

Graham, however, didn't let up in his support of McCarthy and MacArthur. In a newspaper interview in Asheville in 1953 he said, ""Everyone is against communism but very few seem to know the true story of the real plan and purpose of communism. They just never took the time to really study communism ... the people we ought to listen to are those who have had experiences with them—the boys in the POW camps,

Gen. Dean, Gen. MacArthur—we can't sit in an arm chair in some university and try to describe the thing."

Elsewhere in the interview which he conducted "in a chair with one leg draped over its arm," he did describe the thing. "'Communism—is a supernatural power, he said, and gets its power from the Devil. Christianity is a supernatural power too, and gets its power from the Lord,' he said."

He elaborated, "I think throughout America in almost every part of our life we are infiltrated with communists, whether they are card-carrying or not. I think it is the duty of the American leaders to uncover communism wherever it is found and I think the American people should thank God for those who are trying to uncover communism, and subversion. But unfortunately we seem to have some leaders who are more interested in headlines than they are in communism."

Warming to his subject he continued, "Communism could well be setting the stage for the anti-Christ that's spoken of in the Bible. There have been anti-God movements but never one on the scale of communism. It is a supernatural force of a supernatural power—I think it gets its power from the devil. I think we ought to build the greatest military power the world has ever seen—quit giving our millions away to all these other countries which are infiltrated with communism, start building a great spiritual program and deal with communism on a spiritual and psychological level."[48]

Speaking at an Armistice Day gathering during the two-week crusade, Graham announced, "World War can start at any time ... we must look to the teachings of Jesus to avert that holocaust."[49] Turning the other cheek did not seem to figure in his interpretation of those teachings.

"The spectacle of what is called religion, or at any rate organized religion, in India and elsewhere, has filled me with horror and I have frequently condemned it and wished to make a clean sweep of it. Almost always it seemed to stand for blind belief and reaction, dogma and bigotry, superstition, exploitation and the preservation of vested interests."

~Jawarhal Nehru

Chapter 4
Sinful Unions

During 1952 Graham made his first contact with oil man and submachine gun manufacturer Russell Maguire, a business operator of tarnished repute, having lost his Wall Street broker's license for what the SEC called "flagrant violations." At the time he entered Graham's world, Maguire had just purchased *The American Mercury* and was rapidly shifting the once-reputable magazine into an anti-Semitic, anti-communist and racist publication.

During a visit to Maguire's palatial home in Palm Beach, Graham turned down the magnate's proposal to sponsor a nationwide crusade, saying, "Mr. Maguire, I can't tell you how much I appreciate that, but we're getting in fifteen-thousand, twenty-five thousand letters every week in our office up in Minneapolis -- every one of them with a dollar or two ... If word were to get out that you were actually underwriting my work, I'm afraid we'd lose that support ..."[50] Instead, Graham suggested that underwriting his film projects would be most helpful. Not long afterward, Maguire sent him $75,000.

Graham's estimate of his postal receipts alone, $25,000 per week, translates to $194,000 weekly in 2007 dollars.[51] That's $8.1 million per year, a tidy tax-free sum for an "evangelistic association" which had only been formalized for one year. By 2004 BGEA's reported annual receipts would swell to $109,608,803 with net assets totaling $271,370,731. Nor does this include magazine, film, TV, radio, property management or advertising companies associated with the ministry.

Graham would reportedly never accept more than a "modest" annual salary, eschewing speakers' fees and honoraria —in 1995, *Christianity Today* pegged his salary at $135,000. But by 2005 his personal compensation package from BGEA exceeded $500,000 per year, according to tax returns filed with the Internal Revenue Service. He also bragged to biographers that since the beginning of his ministry he had "never paid for a hotel room or a suit." There are other ways to support a ministry beyond checks in the collection plate.

Graham's outreach to oil magnates and arms industrialists went well beyond concern for their souls. As detailed by historian Kevin Phillips in *American Theocracy,* the latter half of the 20th century saw a growing consonance between the goals of evangelical Christians and America's petroleum czars. Oil money would play no small part in Graham's expanding ministry.

Nor did the supplicant preacher arrive with entirely empty pockets. He had thousands of radio listeners. By 1953, Graham's *Hour of Decision* program enjoyed a national audience which learned that the Garden of Eden was a place with "no union dues, no labor leaders, no snakes, no disease." According to biographer Marshall Frady, "He also indicated that any Christian laborer 'would not stoop to take unfair advantage' of his employer by aligning himself with a union."[52] As Phillips wryly noted, "Economic conservatives often warm to sects in which a preoccupation with personal salvation turns lower-income persons away from distracting visions of economic and social reform."[53]

War was another frequent theme in Graham's bombast. He described the conflict between communism and Christianity as "a battle to the death -- either communism must die, or Christianity must die, because it is actually a battle between Christ and Anti-Christ."[54] And when he reproduced this opinion in the pages of *The American Mercury* he added, "Satan began his revolution in the Garden of Eden. With Cain as the first devout follower, and with his brother Abel as a blood sacrifice to totalitarianism, he has slaughtered, plundered and bludgeoned his way through the centuries."[55]

During his 1953 Asheville crusade he quoted Eisenhower to the effect that "I am convinced that America must have a religious revival if America is to be saved." He continued, "Secretary of State John Foster Dulles told me the same thing a few days ago. Our Army generals have been warning us that the enemy can now penetrate this nation with atomic power that could destroy and cripple us within 24 hours."[56]

Graham's anti-communist, anti-labor pitch fit well with the politics of several of his political allies, most particularly the red-scare tactics of Senator Lyndon Baines Johnson and a young congressman named Richard Milhaus Nixon. These early right-wing allies would be joined in due time by the union-bashing Ronald Reagan and his legatees, the Georges Bush.

Eisenhower, progenitor of the Interstate Highway system, was no stranger to the power of oil and internal combustion manufacturing interests. As Richardson's active involvement in recruiting clearly suggests, he was the candidate of the oil lobby. While he advanced the highway plan under the aegis of defense, as a means to move a motorized army in response to invasion, General Eisenhower moved in tandem with General Motors. As Nixon would remark in *Six Crises,* "Eisenhower was a far more complex and devious man than most people realized, and in the best sense of those words."

Thus, Graham's presidential politics aligned perfectly with the goals of Chrysler, Ford and GM, who had made it their business to derail public transportation. Phillips elaborates, "... during the 1930s, 1940s, and 1950s the auto-making big three worked to push the U.S. transportation system into car dependence. Led by GM, the automakers acquired bus manufacturers and lines, then promoted diesel buses to displace both intercity rail transportation and electric transit systems."[57]

As mid-term elections hove into view, Graham wrote Ike in February, 1954: "Saturday night I heard Congressman Walter Judd address the Lincoln Day Dinner here in Asheville. He spoke for an hour and a half and gave the most logical and dynamic presentation and defense of your administration that I have ever heard. I told him afterward that if he could give that same address on all the Television networks, we wouldn't have to worry about Congress remaining GOP controlled this fall."[58]

Three months later he wrote, "I have been praying for you in the last few days as you wrestle with the Indo-China problem. Whatever your ultimate decision, I shall do my best through radio and television to make my contribution in selling the American public."[59]

Dien Bien Phu, a French base, had just been overrun by the Communists, and despite urging from Dulles, the Joint Chiefs and Vice President Nixon, Eisenhower refrained from sending in U.S. forces.

Regarding such wrestling, historian Seth Jacobs reported that Eisenhower was clearly influenced by that era's religious revival in the United States the following year when he installed Ngo Dinh Diem, a devout Catholic, as head of the South Vietnamese government -- despite Diem's unpopularity and incompetence.[60]

In a further measure of "religious" outreach to the region, Ike assigned Secretary of State John Foster Dulles to brief Graham on Indian politics and relations between the United States and India shortly before his 1956 crusade there. Graham later wrote that Dulles was particularly keen to inform him about recent visits to the subcontinent by Nikita Kruschev and Nikolai Bulganin who were working to improve India's relationship with the Soviet Union.

When Ike made his reelection bid later that year, Graham's active support continued. He wrote, "I shall do all in my power during the coming campaign to gain friends and supporters for your cause."

Eisenhower forwarded the letter to Leonard W. Hall, Chairman of the Republican National Committee on Sept. 3, with an addendum: "It occurs to me that some time during the campaign we might want to call on him for a little help."[61]

Notwithstanding his support for Eisenhower, Graham sometimes swerved far to the right of the President. Republican Senator Joseph McCarthy's anticommunist witch-hunt came in for particular praise and Graham heartily endorsed McCarthy's proposal that Fifth Amendment protection be stripped from those he accused of communist sympathies—"Let's do it!"[62] was his helpful addition to the debate.

Ike was not persuaded and instructed Nixon to attack McCarthy. Nixon did so in a speech delivered on March 4, 1954. Though he didn't mention McCarthy by name, the veil was thin as he used his own communist bashing reputation to take down the Senator: "Men who have in the past done effective work exposing Communists in this country have, by reckless talk and questionable methods, made themselves the issue rather than the cause they believe in so deeply."

Others took up the task of correcting the wayward witch hunter. Though McCarthy's initial attacks had particularly targeted New Deal Democrats, the Wisconsin Senator's excesses eventually embarrassed many in his own party. On December 2, 1954, a bipartisan censure motion condemned his conduct by 67 votes to 22.

Graham's support for McCarthy didn't waver. He condemned the Senate, not the Senator, and said the censure lent "disgrace to the dignity of American statesmanship."[63]

"In London on the south coast of England, every day except Sunday, they carry from the sewage system of London a shipload of a poisonous substance that would destroy—or just a few drops of it—would destroy anything. They carry it from the disposal plants. Then they take it about twenty miles to where the sea is one of the deepest spots in the world, and they dump it all out of the ship into the sea. But within twenty minutes that water is as pure as when they put this poisonous substance in it."

~ **Billy Graham**
Sermon, Charlotte Crusade
Sept. 27, 1958

Chapter 5
Mysterious Change

In 1954, Graham's political zeal caused a furor in Britain, the first stop on a European crusade. A pamphlet printed at BGEA's Minneapolis headquarters and distributed to London churchmen contained a sentence attributed to Graham which read, "What Hitler's bombs could not do, socialism with its accompanying evils, shortly accomplished." Britain's socialist Labor Party supporters took umbrage, and Graham rapidly backpedaled, with the claim that, "One word mysteriously got changed ...," and an insistence that someone else in his ministry had substituted the word "socialism" for "secularism." The British press was not impressed, however, and the early days of the London crusade were focussed on damage control during openly hostile press conferences.[64]

No matter who inserted the word "socialism" into that particular text, it was clearly on-message. Graham's rhetoric was filled with anticommunist and antisocialist zeal. He told a California crusade that Karl Marx was a "degenerate materialist," whose perverse philosophy embraced the "filthy, corrupt, ungodly, unholy doctrine of world socialism." In line with his support for McCarthy, "Graham called for 'internal security' investigations to expose the 'pinks, the lavenders and the reds who have sought refuge beneath the wings of the American eagle.'"[65]

In recalling his mood during his fire-and-brimstone declamations, Graham said, "I would feel as though I had a sword, a rapier, in my hand, and I would be slashing deeper and deeper into the consciences of the people before me, cutting away straight to their very souls."[66]

Nor did he spare the rod, at least in theory, during his occasional visits home. In 1969 he described his parenting technique to *Good Housekeeping* magazine. "I had to spank them sometimes, but on each occasion, I talked to them first for ten or fifteen minutes, explaining their transgressions. Next I read the Bible to them. Finally I punished them. Our daughters got the same treatment."[67] Years later, one daughter would contradict her father's reports, saying that Ruth had been the administrator of "whippings" with all regimentation dropped during Graham's infrequent appearances.

He might have been harkening back to his own childhood beatings which his father administered with a broad leather belt. The confrontations were so violent, according to Graham's autobiography, that he once kicked back and broke two of his father's ribsa. His mother was somewhat less violent, relying on a long hickory switch to "whistle" her children. She later recalled, "Perhaps we were both a little too strict, perhaps we whipped them more than we should have."[68] Biographer Marshall Frady reports, "Billy was systematically drilled by his mother in such Old Testament verses as 'For we are consumed by Thine anger, and by Thy wrath are we troubled. Thou hast set our iniquities before Thee, our secret sins in the light of Thy countenance. ...'"

Confirming his sister's remembrance, Franklin later wrote that their mother Ruth had used a wide leather belt to administer beatings. And Ruth told Frady, "I played them like a xylophone."

If the Graham family's child-rearing theories trended to the corporal, Graham's prescription for youth in general was no less disciplined. During a crusade in 1958 he proclaimed, "All over this world tonight, young people are seeking security. They want a master! They want a center of life! I believe Jesus Christ can become that master! Just as Hitler was able to get the youth of Germany, and Mussolini was able to get the youth of Italy, and the Communists were able to get the youth of Eastern Europe!"[69]

In his autobiography, Graham reminisces about his excitement listening to Hitler's radio broadcasts. Though the youth didn't understand a word of German, the dictator's rhythm and fervor struck a chord. "I was particularly fascinated by the oratorical style of speeches shouted in an almost hypnotic voice by a man in Germany named Adolf Hitler."[70]

Biographer Frady reported on the fervor of Graham's late 50's anticommunism. "In October of 1957, he announced that he had it 'on good authority' that a faction in the Kremlin was demanding an attack on the U.S. within two years, and in 1960, declared that Soviet submarines were 'sitting off our coast with atomic warheads on their rockets that can penetrate fifteen hundred miles.'"[71]

It was during the early 50's that Graham decided to publish a magazine. By his account he climbed out of bed in the middle of a night in late 1953 and sketched out plans for a publication that would "give theological respectability to evangelicals."[72] By the time the idea reached fruition in 1956 he had decided to site its headquarters in Washington, D.C., both to keep tabs on and to influence public policy.

Christianity Today would become a powerful instrument in the battle for control of modern Protestantism, and Graham would keep an ink-stained finger in its affairs through the next four decades, at one point installing his father-in-law, L. Nelson Bell as executive editor.

Graham's 1957 Madison Square Garden crusade was very successful — he generated a profit of $217,000 over the course of sixteen weeks—that's $1,587,000 in 2007 dollars. Fifty thousand of those dollars came in the form of a single check from John D. Rockefeller, Jr., and while spiritual salvation may have been one motive for such generosity, access to South American oil fields was another. Perhaps more important than the Rockefeller's financial infusion was introduction to Nelson Rockefeller's foreign policy wunderkind, Henry Kissinger. Kissinger would interact with Graham through at least five presidential administrations.

The web of connections between Graham, missionaries working in oil- and mineral-rich regions of South America, the genocide of more than 100,000 indigenous people, the CIA, and the Rockefellers is tangled—for full documentation, see Gerard Colby's 960-page account, *Thy Will be Done* [73]. The result, however, was very simple: land populated by natives who did not welcome miners or oil rigs was depopulated. Stalled development moved forward.

Standard Oil and Shell Oil had led the way into Huaorani territory in Ecuador's Amazon region and had been driven out in 1948 by indigenous tribes weary of enslavement and massacre by rubber barons. Spears and poison darts convinced the oil companies to pack it in, a retreat considerably eased by a simultaneous decision to focus on oil reserves in the Mideast made more available by Allied success in the recent World War.

A more fruitful South American invasion was held together by the Missionary Aviation Fellowship which flew supplies to Christian missions that were advancing into the region. Others were linked by the Jungle Aviation and Radio Service (JAARS), formed by two Graham backers and underwritten by Quaker Oats heir (and Moody Bible Institute vice president) Henry Coleman Cromwell. JAARS and many of the missions were also connected to Cameron Townsend's Summer Institute of Linguistics (SIL), whose academic name belied fundamentalist missionary roots — an aura useful in places where religion was less politically palatable than research. SIL was a front organization for Wycliffe Bible Translators which translated bibles into native tongues. At the same time, SIL provided translation services for the CIA in Latin America and later Vietnam, and acted to silence Indian voices when corporations and U.S. policy wreaked havoc on native populations, ignoring the most basic human rights priniciples and international law.

Wycliffe/SIL political intrigue is explored in exhaustive detail in *Fishers of Men or Founders of Empire,* by anthropologist David Stoll, a book which independently affirms much of Colby's reporting. The dense volume, a result of seven years of research, demonstrates that the organization has destroyed indigenous culture and advanced U.S. imperialism in developing countries around the globe. Concerning Peru, Stoll wrote, "Here and elsewhere, SIL's fortunes not only revolved around the relations between a foreign government and its own: as Bible translation came to resemble a paramilitary operation, no government would tolerate it without close ties with Washington."[74] Stoll notes further that during the rise of the Townsend ministries the U.S. Government organized a peacetime foreign espionage arm called the Office of Strategic Services. He reports, "[C]hartered as the Central Intelligence Agency in 1947, it would make extensive use of missionaries."[75] Furthermore, "The evangelical opinion leader *Christianity Today* considered Wycliffe's success second only to that of Billy Graham."[76]

Colby reported that SIL was instrumental in killing the story of the bloody 1954 U.S. invasion of Guatemala, when Eisenhower, Secretary of State John Foster Dulles and CIA Director Allen Dulles took exception to the democratic election of the reformist Jacobo Arbenz. Arbenz had won the first-ever universal-sufferage election in Guatemala's history with promises to make the nation an economically independent, capitalist state and to shed its colonial dependence on the U.S. He soon instituted land reform with a plan modeled on the United States' Homestead Act, providing about one hundred thousand landless peasants with a stake in the country's future by purchasing unused arable land for the tax value claimed by private owners and granting peasants title to it.

Oddly, the corporate owners were incensed that offered prices were so impossibly low. Arbenz also made the mistake of proposing a modest tax on bananas, that being the country's only significant export. In a pattern that would become familiar in Cuba, Nicaragua, Chile and Peru, the U.S. sided with the disempowered colonial elite and provided weapons to guerillas, perhaps more accurately described as mercenaries. The United Fruit Company, a major player in the Guatemalan economy with close ties to the Dulles brothers' law firm, abetted the putsch. The Arbenz government was soon replaced with a military junta, ushering in a decades-long period of dictatorial rule and bloody suppression of indigenous freedom fighters.

That Graham's magazine, *Christianity Today,* extolled Wycliffe's success should come as no surprise since Graham later sat on the Wycliffe board and maintains close ties to the organization to the present time. And Dulles, as we have seen, was in close touch with Graham. Later, *Time* magazine would report that Graham's work in South America had been partly underwritten by an organization funded directly by the C.I.A.

"All gods who receive homage are cruel. All gods dispense cruelty without reason. Otherwise they would not be worshipped. ... Half gods are worshipped in wine and flowers. Real gods require blood."

~ Zora Neale Hurston
Their Eyes Were Watching God

Chapter 6
Matters of Faith

A Missionary Aviation Fellowship plane disappeared in Ecuador in 1955 while on a mission and Billy Graham's Jungle Aviation And Radio Service team was first to arrive. They found the hacked and mutilated bodies of four of the five missionaries floating in the Curaray River, with native spears protruding from their bodies. The plane had been heavily damaged as well. Two weeks later Luce published photos in *Life* with a thrilling story of the martyrs' deaths, purportedly refusing to use their weapons on their attackers. The story gripped the nation. Nixon and Truman helped arrange donations of planes (to be operated by the Summer Institute of Linguistics or SIL) to governments in Latin America for "pacification" work. The U.S. base of operations was provided by Graham's cohort.

Rachel Saint, the sister of the pilot, was also a missionary and she insisted on continuing her work with the natives. When she traveled to the U.S. in 1957, accompanied by Dayuma, her Huaorani translator, she created a sensation on TV and in an appearance at Graham's Madison Square Garden crusade—a woman so devoted to her mission that she forgave her brothers' killers. During the crusade, word reached Dayuma that the "martyred missionaries" had killed Huaoranis including her relatives on that remote riverside, but the inconvenient fact of bullet-riddled native bodies was buried and Dayuma's rage was kept secret until she was safely out of the country.

One of the tactics used by missionaries was to fly over villages targeted for salvation, dropping candy, small gifts and pictures of the white people who would shortly make an appearance. Soon these tactics were adopted by mercenaries who would make two passes, the first to drop sugar to collect denizens in a village, the second to drop dynamite. Later, after native defense of territory was redefined as communist insurgency, the

U.S. government supplied napalm which had the added benefit of incinerating evidence of genocide.

The line between mercenaries, military and missionaries was blurred. SIL-operated planes were incorporated into national air forces that participated in genocidal attacks. Missionary maps were used for targeting and SIL's description of various tribes as "hostile" or "warlike" was relayed to government agencies. The Huaorani were particularly fierce and were also known in the region as the Aucas, a Quichua word for savages. At least nine tribes first contacted by SIL were subsequently exterminated.

"South-east of Lago Agrio, in what is now the Auca oil field, the Summer Institute removed most of the people from the land which the government had leased to North American oil companies. ... At their height, the removals met with no challenge because the plans of everyone from the Gulf and Texaco oil corporations to the Lowland Quichua depended on subduing or exterminating the Huaorani."[77]

With Rockefeller's oil development opponents eliminated, contributions flowed to SIL, Wycliffe and the Graham crusades. In 1958 the Graham organization was able to procure a U.S. base of operations for JAARS in Charlotte.

According to Vernon William Patterson, a leader in evangelistic activities in Charlotte during that era, "In the '58 crusade of Billy, Henderson Belk and his wife went forward and accepted Christ and became very zealous for Christian work." Soon, according to Patterson, Graham persuaded Henderson Belk to provide land for a new JAARS headquarters.[78] Belk arranged use of a former Army base and later an abandoned plantation as the stateside air base. Belk was a department store magnate who was busy assembling a billion dollar fortune with the help of Rockefeller's Chase Manhattan Bank.

Billy Graham remained closely tied to Wycliffe/SIL and the Jungle Aviation and Radio Service. He sat on the Wycliffe board from about 1958 until 1961 when he quit in a dispute over the founder's fundraising tactics, but BGEA continued to provide funds to Wycliffe well into the 21st Century. As documented by material in the Billy Graham folder in the Johnson library, Ruth Bell Graham's minister in Montreat, Rev. Calvin Thielman, took

Cameron Townsend to Vietnam in 1967 as part of a presidentially sanctioned tour. Familial ties remain strong and Franklin Graham's Samaritan's Purse organizations continue to work with Missionary Aviation Fellowship and JAARS.

In the months preceding the 1960 presidential election Graham played a significant role in fomenting anti-Catholicism in order to boost Nixon's chances against Kennedy—at least until it became clear that the anti-Catholic bigotry issue was working in Kennedy's favor. At that juncture, Graham quickly altered his rhetoric.

Early in that election season Graham made statements to reporters such as: "A man's religion cannot be separated from his person: therefore, where religion involves political decisions, it becomes a legitimate issue." And, "Some Protestants are hesitant about voting for a Catholic because the Catholic church is not only a religious, but a secular institution which sends and receives ambassadors from secular states." At the same time, Graham was arranging speaking engagements for Nixon in front of large religious groups including national conclaves of Presbyterians and Southern Baptists. In addition he hosted a private luncheon in Montreat where Nixon met with leaders of the Presbyterian, Episcopal, Methodist and Southern Baptist churches.[79]

A group of conservative Protestants calling themselves Citizens for Religious Freedom fomented anti-Catholic sentiment, and Graham was very close to its organizers. The group had formed following a meeting of evangelicals called by Graham in Montreux, Switzerland. When the Citizens for Religious Freedom held their first public event in Washington, Graham stayed away, but Norman Vincent Peale, Nelson Bell and others had taken up the cause. As reported by *Time* magazine, "Dr. L. Nelson Bell, executive editor of the biweekly *Christianity Today* (paid and free circ.: 160,000) and father-in-law of Billy Graham, was more alarmed. Too many Protestants, said he, are 'soft' on Catholicism. 'Pseudo tolerance is not tolerance at all but simply ignorance.' If Jack Kennedy were to become President, he said, then Montana's Mike Mansfield would become Senate majority leader and Massachusetts' John W. McCormack would continue as House Democratic floor leader. 'Both are fine men, but both belong to a church with headquarters in Rome.' And to

Bell, Rome was little better than Moscow: 'The antagonism of the Roman church to Communism is in part because of similar methods.'"[80] At the same time, "The president of the Southern Baptist Convention [Graham's church] declared that he was not being a bigot when he said, 'All we ask is that Roman Catholicism lift its bloody hand from the throats of those that want to worship in the church of their choice.'"[81]

Christianity Today ran an unsigned editorial advising readers that it was "perfectly rational" for Protestants to oppose election of a Catholic. "Where the Romanists are strong enough, they persecute. Where less strong, they oppress and harrass; where they are in the minority, they seek special privileges, Government favor and more power."[82]

When the anti-Catholic effort resulted in excoriating attacks from columnists, editorial writers and a host of mainstream politicians, Graham insisted, "I wasn't necessarily involved. Norman Vincent Peale was involved."[83] However, Grady Wilson, Graham's lifelong lieutenant, told a radio audience that a midnight mass had been held where Catholics prayed that the military plane carrying Graham to Spain would crash.[84]

Later Graham would write Nixon that he was "detaching himself from some of the cheap religious bigotry and diabolical whisperings that are going on," and, "You must continue to stay a million miles from the religious issue at this time."[85] Graham had another election plan for Nixon, involving what would come to be known decades later as "wagging the dog." He urged Nixon to stake out a critical position concerning Cuba's move toward communism. Then "Graham recommended that Nixon urge the President to take some dramatic action, perhaps even to break diplomatic relations with Cuba." Nixon took the advice seriously and told his aides, "I think this makes a hell of a lot of sense. ... Please note the paragraph where he is talking about the Cuban situation. I would like you Len [Hall], to go over and have a chat with the President about that situation. I don't know whether anything can be done about it, but it does show what his reactions are."[86]

The Bay of Pigs invasion, whose failure was laid at Kennedy's feet, was initially plotted by Nixon, military leaders and the CIA during Eisenhower's tenure. Whether Graham's letter actually instigated the plan or was merely one more supportive voice for intervention is not clear from the record.

Following Nixon's nomination at the 1960 Republican National Convention, Graham wrote a letter marked "strictly confidential" to Eisenhower: "Your speech to the convention was absolutely superb. This is the kind of fighting speech I hope you will continue to give. I am convinced that the next six months can be the most crucial and decisive of your entire career. You are the one person that the American people will listen to. I hope that you will stump the country making this type of speech on behalf of Nixon ... I believe that Nixon has a fighting chance only if you go all out. I know this would mean two months of hard work, but I believe the rewards to the Nation would be as great as when you led the armies at Normandy.

"It is also my opinion that you must win the battle in the coming special session of Congress. It seems to me that you could send so many dramatic messages to Congress that you could keep Kennedy and Johnson off-balance and capture the headlines during that period."[87]

Throughout his career, Graham maintained a pro forma posture of political neutrality while actively campaigning for his chosen candidates. In 1960 when his longtime friend was closing in on the Republican nomination for the presidency, the minister wrote Nixon a letter advocating the choice of Dr. Walter Judd as a running mate. (Judd was a former evangelical minister and, at that time, a U.S. Representative.)

"With Dr. Judd, I believe the two of you could present a picture to America that would put much of the South and border states in the Republican column and bring about a dedicated Protestant vote to counteract the Catholic vote."

"I would appreciate your considering this letter in utter confidence," he continued. "You would do me a favor by destroying it after reading it."[88]

Obsessively concerned with creation of a historical record of his presidency, Nixon was not in the habit of destroying documents or tapes—a practice which caught up with the President and others, including Graham, many years later. In the event, Judd was offered the vice presidential nomination and declined.

At the urging of Henry Luce, Graham then wrote an article for *Life* magazine praising Nixon and making it clear that he endorsed Nixon, with a string of thinly veiled attacks on Kennedy. He stated that voters shouldn't choose a presidential candidate who is "more handsome or charming" or who "happened to be richer." Kennedy got wind of the story and demanded that, in fairness, Luce should run a companion piece by one of Kennedy's religious supporters, perhaps Reinhold Neibuhr. Luce pulled the story and Graham was elated. He had developed a case of cold feet, and, when Luce decided to go ahead with the story the following week, Graham withdrew the article and substituted a nonpartisan article on why Christians should vote.[89]

Graham did not hold Kennedy in high regard and said, "Kennedy was no intellectual—I mean, he was written up by the eastern press as an intellectual because he agreed with the eastern establishment. But Nixon is a true intellectual and he is a student, particularly a student of history."[90]

Quite apart from Graham's low regard for Kennedy and their electoral political differences, the two men were at odds on two of the greatest issues of the day: the necessity of a military show-down with communism and government action regarding racial integration.

"For years now I have heard the word 'Wait!' ... This 'Wait' has almost always meant 'Never.' We must come to see, with one of our distinguished jurists, that 'Justice delayed is justice denied.'"

~Martin Luther King, Jr.
Letter from Birmingham Jail

Chapter 7
Versus Kennedy and King

Given Graham's support of Nixon in the 1960 election, and his strenuous effort to keep a Catholic out of the White House, it is no surprise that relations with Kennedy were strained from the outset. However, the president-elect was advised by an astute political operative—his father, Ambassador Joseph Kennedy—to make an overture to the powerful evangelist.

Five days before the inauguration, Kennedy took Graham golfing in Palm Beach, discussed matters of faith with his erstwhile opponent and took him for a spin in his convertible. While the meeting was polite, relations remained cool and there was little contact between the preacher and the White House during Kennedy's abbreviated presidency. In his 1997 autobiography, Graham claimed that he had had a premonition concerning Kennedy's assassination which also, oddly, invoked golf.

"I unaccountably felt such a burden about the presidential visit to Dallas that I decided to phone our mutual friend, Senator [George] Smathers, to tell him I really wanted to talk to the president." Smathers was on the Senate floor, and unavailable, so Graham left a message with his secretary. For some reason, Smathers thought the message concerned rescheduling a golf game and sent him a telegram to the effect that Kennedy would contact Graham directly. Kennedy never called. Graham wrote, "But all I wanted to tell him and the president was one thing, 'Don't go to Texas!'"[91]

Kennedy had grave reservations about the Bay of Pigs invasion, plotted by the CIA under Eisenhower, but was assured by Allen Dulles and Richard Bissell of that agency that the plan would quickly succeed. It would be four decades before declassified documents showed that the plotters expected to trap Kennedy into full U.S. military support for the invasion. Keenly attuned to world opinion and particularly that of Latin American nations weary of North American intervention in their political affairs, and aware that the Soviet Union could make a counter move in Berlin, Kennedy demurred. He took the heat for failure, but fired Dulles.

A year and a half later, when saber-rattling between the two super-powers came to a head as the Soviet Union placed nuclear armed missiles in Cuba in response to U.S. deployment of similar arms in Turkey, the CIA and Joint Chiefs of Staff urged Kennedy toward war. Air Force chief General Curtis LeMay urged a pre-emptive nuclear strike against Russia while the U.S. still held a massive arms superiority. He encouraged Kennedy to "fry" Cuba. Kennedy resisted and negotiated an end to the impasse through direct and indirect communication with Soviet Premier Nikita Kruschev. Once again, declassified documents would prove Kennedy right—forty years on. Then it was learned that operational nuclear missiles were in place and ready to fire and that Soviet commanders in Cuba had full authorization to unleash those weapons against the U.S. mainland if we had attacked. Had Kennedy pursued the beligerant course advised by his generals, the southeastern states would have been reduced to a radioactive wasteland, proving the truth of Kennedy's memorable phrase concerning a "worldwide nuclear war in which even the fruits of victory would be ashes in our mouth."

Graham was holding a crusade in Buenos Aires during most of the eleven days in October, 1962, when the Cuban missile crisis unfolded. In his sermons he reportedly took the military's line, urging a confrontation with the Soviets. Oddly, considering the Graham Archive's hyper-documentation of Graham's every sore throat, luncheon, sermon or press conference, no transcripts of those sermons are available in Wheaton.

While Kennedy fully supported an arms build-up, advocating "peace through strength," he believed that military strength made diplomacy possible. In regard to Vietnam, some sources report he told close associates that following reelection in 1964 he intended to withdraw all 16,000 United States soldiers from Vietnam, once again differing with Graham who would become a vociferous supporter of war in Southeast Asia.

Concerning race relations, Kennedy and Graham were equally at odds, though Graham worked hard later to reframe his position as popular opinion gradually moved toward acceptance of racial justice. After the fact, Graham claimed to have been a staunch opponent of segregation in the first decade of his fame and variously claimed to have torn down the ropes between black and white seating at either his 1952 Jackson, Mississippi, crusade or his 1953 Chattanooga, Tennessee, event, with Chattanooga becoming the set piece over time. All references to his putative action are in Graham's own sermons and writing; there are no extant news reports of the gesture. Perhaps reporters ignored it due to the systemic racism of the era or overlooked his action due to lack of response on the part of attendees.

Whatever the case may be, later that year in Asheville, North Carolina, Graham held a whites-only crusade. Civil rights activist Oralene Graves Simmons recalls the anger felt within the city's black community, an anger she says lingers to this day. "I'm sure many black folks had sent Billy Graham money, but they weren't welcome at the Civic Center. When he was asked about it afterward, Graham said it wasn't his decision but that of the organizers."

During the whole of his fourteen day Asheville event the daily paper carried only one mention of the whites-only policy and that in a letter to the editor. Nor was there any follow-up coverage. In her letter to the *Asheville Citizen-Times*, Mrs. E.L. Knick lamented, "Why have the so-called church workers and Christians of our city barred the colored people from the Billy Graham revival? I am interested in knowing who is responsible." Later she observes, "My Bible tells me the message is for all, regardless of religion or color. I know, in that crowd at the Auditorium, there are people of every religion and nationality. Why make an example of the Negro because of the color of his skin? Is not his soul as important as yours and mine?"[92]

No answer was forthcoming from the paper then, or in the weeks that followed.

Knick's query was thrown into sharper relief by Graham's sermonizing which the daily reprinted verbatim, day-by-day through the two week residency. On November 16, eight days into the crusade, Graham told the audience, "At the foot of the cross there is no racial barrier, no color barrier. We stand naked in the sight of God." There was evidently a failure of communication with the front office—blacks were not admitted.[93]

Asheville native Dr. John P. Holt, a retired African-American physician, didn't particularly fault Graham for his whites-only events in the 50s. "That was the rule of things. We had separate everything." Holt spent the late 1940s and 50s at Western Reserve University, the University of Michigan at Ann Arbor, Brown University and Columbia Medical School before circling back home. "By the time I returned to Asheville in 1961, it was a big thing for the Graham events to let blacks come and sit in the gallery." That is to say, blacks were up in the balcony where white participants wouldn't be forced to see them.

William Martin, probably the most authoritative biographical source, offers quotes from Graham that put him at diametric odds with integrationists, calling segregation a "local" problem and denying any Biblical support for King's work. In *A Prophet With Honor,* Martin wrote, "That summer in Jackson, Mississippi, in the heart of the black belt, he accepted segregated seating but defied Governor Hugh White's request that he hold entirely separate services for blacks. ... Near the close of the crusade, Graham took another step by not only proclaiming God's love knows no racial barriers but by identifying Jackson's two greatest social problems as illegal liquor (Mississippi was still dry) and segregation.

"[W]hen segregationists criticized him, he immediately backtracked. He told the local newspaper, 'I feel I have been misrepresented on racial segregation. We follow the existing social customs in whatever part of the country in which we minister. As far as I have been able to find in my study of the Bible, it has nothing to say about segregation or non-segregation. I came to Jackson to preach only the Bible and not to enter into local issues.' Just one day earlier, preaching the Bible required that segregation be condemned and characterized the practice as on a par with bootlegger's moonshine, only one rung lower than immorality on the ladder of major sins. When it appeared that such a message might shrink the size of his potential audience, Graham decided that it was no longer 'unscriptural' but simply a 'local issue.'"[94]

Emblematic of Graham's careful dance concerning integration was his advice to Eisenhower prior to the 1956 presidential race. Eisenhower had written him to as that he enlist ministers to advance the cause of desegration on moral grounds.

Graham's immediate response was that he would gather major southern religious leaders and see what he could do. But politics seemed to trump morality when he added, "Immediately after the election you can take whatever steps you feel are wise and right. In the meantime, it might be well to let the Democratic party bear the brunt of the debate."[95]

In 2001, the Asheville *Citizen-Times* quoted Graham in its coffee table encomium, *A Portrait of Billy Graham:* "One of the things I accomplished was pulling down the ropes that segregated the crowd in Chattanooga in 1952 [sic]. Blacks came in large numbers and usually sat with other blacks, but they were free to sit where they wanted."[96] Three pages later, the same volume contradicts that memory, stating, "To his disappointment, though, black attendance was small and those that came tended to sit together rather than mingle with whites."[97]

Drawing on a 1986 Graham sermon, Martin reported the same, "In fact, few blacks dared to move into the white sections, and many people may not have realized what Graham had done— the incident passed without comment in local papers—but he could not know what might happen, and the gesture was significant. In Dallas, a few months later, he backslid a bit by accepting the sponsoring committee's designation of separate seating areas for blacks and whites."[98]

Then, in Martin's most telling observation he notes, "After the Supreme Court decision on May 17, 1954, he no longer permitted any form of enforced segregation at his meetings, even in the Deep South, though he sometimes seemed less concerned with the intrinsic injustice of racial discrimination than with the effect on his ministry's image."[99] Concern with image is the most plausible reason why he invited Martin Luther King, Jr., to offer an opening prayer for his 1957 New York City crusade, an invitation that netted Graham severe criticism from old guard southern religionists while scoring points in more progressive circles, not least of all for Nixon who also attended the New York event. Once again he could be seen to be adhering to local custom. However that may be, neither image nor concern about injustice convinced Graham to take any substantive action outside of his meetings.

As late as 1991 Graham maintained an active membership in the then-discriminatory Biltmore Forest Country Club which had gone so far as to eject a black child from its pool in 1988, though the little boy was the guest of a member. When confronted by WNC activist Monroe Gilmour, Graham's office responded that he "didn't have time to involve himself in local issues." Thanks to persistent inquiries from Gilmour and his organization, WNC Citizens for an End to Institutional Bigotry, the country club "clarified" its formerly unwritten policy concerning race and issued a written non-discrimination statement.

Later in 1957, three years after the Brown v. Board of Education decision, a federal court ordered the Little Rock, Ark., school system to integrate. Governor Orval Faubus defied the court, calling in the National Guard to prevent nine black teenagers from entering the city's high school. Ten days later he met with President Eisenhower and agreed to use the National Guard to protect the students; but on returning to Little Rock he dismissed the troops, leaving the teens to face an angry white, brick-throw++ng mob. After school doors and windows were smashed and several reporters beaten, local police were forced to evacuate the nine students.

Graham was asked by other spiritual and secular leaders to help calm the city as federal troops imposed integration of the schools, but he demurred. Graham put off going there for more than a year, and later said that decision was made based on Eisenhower's advice. But it clearly avoided possible negative repercussions from his white southern base at a moment when the crisis was front page news.

Moreover, when he finally held a crusade in the embattled city, in September, 1959, he claimed that racists had tried to forestall the show. Former President Bill Clinton would relate Graham's version of events at the dedicatory ceremony for the Billy Graham Library in May, 2007. Clinton said, "The White Citizens Council in Little Rock tried to convince, even to pressure, Billy Graham and all of his people to preach to a segregated audience. Get this, in War Memorial Stadium, our football stadium. And he told them if they insisted on that, he would cancel the crusade and tell the whole world why. They folded like Dick's hatband." Furthermore, Clinton stated that at Graham's crusade, "tens of thousands of black and white Christians there together in a football stadium.... It was the beginning of the end of the old South in my home state."

The problem with Clinton's recitation is not so much fact as spin. Though the city high schools had been closed during the 1958-59 school year they opened a month early the following fall, and were more or less quietly integrating by the time Graham set up camp in the stadium. There were still hard feelings and one student's home had been bombed a month before the event, but the peak of the crisis was past. As for Graham's bold threat to cancel, it is unclear that the White Citizen's Council had any say in whether or not the event would be staged. Another way to view what occurred is that Graham did "tell the world" about alleged pressure. How else did Clinton learn of it? It's a safe bet the WCC didn't publicize the story of how they were supposedly faced down by the brave preacher. Graham thus placed himself in the best possible light and generated positive publicity that still redounded to his benefit five decades later.

Further evidence that the Little Rock event represented business-as-usual for BGEA rather than a pastoral response to a social emergency can be deduced from the timing of Graham's appearance there. In city after city Graham's advance team routinely moved in a year before a planned crusade, create a dedicated corporate entity, contact churches, hold weekly block parties, schedule local entertainers and initiate media contact. Orchestration of a financially successful spectacle requires a substantial commitment of time, whereas the calming appearance of a public figure in the hours of a crisis can be arranged overnight.

In the meantime, Graham planned to hold an event on statehouse grounds in Columbia, South Carolina, 1958, but was blocked by then-Governor George Bell Timmerman who argued that it would violate the separation clause in the U.S. Constitution. Timmerman's actual reason was clearly understood: Graham had stopped permitting segregation of his crusades. The event was moved to nearby Fort Jackson with benefit of the publicity boost garnered from the Governor's decision. In later years this was added to the "proof" that Graham was a staunch supporter of integration.

In October, 2010, Graham supporters staged "Come Together Day" and obtained a proclamation to that effect from Governor Mark Sanford. In that document, Sanford stated that "people will gather with a spirit of unity, a belief in equality and faith that Christian principles will prevail against discrimination and injustice ..." Thanks in no small part to Graham's work through the intervaling years, the separation clause had been discarded, at least where political opportunity offered itself during a heated election season.

Whatever the rationale for his purported opposition to segregation, Graham strongly opposed those who pressed for rapid change in racist laws. Six years further on, in April, 1963, the perceived threat of violence in Birmingham triggered a court injunction aimed at ending peaceful demonstrations there. *Christian Century* magazine editorialized in support of King's decision to ignore the court order and chastised Billy Graham for advising King "to put the brakes on a little bit".[100] Graham's advice had gone out while King was languishing in the Birmingham jail. According to biographer Martin, Graham said King's timing was "questionable" and suggested "that blacks and whites alike would benefit from 'a period of quietness in which moderation prevails.'"[101]

In August, 1963, following Martin Luther King's "I Have a Dream" speech on the steps of the Lincoln Memorial, Graham's response was, "Only when Christ comes again will the little white children of Alabama walk hand in hand with little black children."[102]

Perhaps emblematic of Graham's opposition to King was his flagship magazine's thoroughgoing avoidance of the man and his work. Though King had been acknowledged as a leader of national stature in the civil rights movement from the mid-fifties forward, *Christianity Today* did not even mention King by name until early 1964, when two sentences announced he had been named *Time's* "Man of the Year."

After passage of the landmark Civil Rights Act that year, Graham publicly appealed to King to stop demonstrating while "the people of the North and West have an opportunity to digest the new Civil Rights Act."[103] And his response to riots across the country was a demand that Congress drop all other work to fashion "new tough laws."[104]

At the same time, Johnson appealed to Graham to sit on a blue ribbon panel, the Community Relations Service, which he had created to handle fall-out from the sweeping legislation. There was serious concern within the administration that the new law could generate a flood of legal challenges and reactionary violence. Graham declined to serve, preferring to focus his efforts on new crusades.

While Graham hid his alleged integrationist candle under a bushel of Biblical excuses, other white religionists laid their beliefs on the line. As far back as 1947, while Graham was launching his national ministry, Rev. Charles Jones had faced down rock-throwing, club-wielding white supremacists and murder threats when he permitted mixed-race labor meetings in his Chapel Hill church. The lunch counter sit-ins in North Carolina in 1960 had drawn support from the North Carolina Council on Human Relations and the Unitarian Fellowship for Social Justice. George Schermer, executive director of the Philadelphia Commission on Human Relations, spoke out in support of rolling boycotts of segregationist businesses organized by the city's black preachers. In 1961, The Rev. William Sloan Coffin, Jr., was arrested in Montgomery, Alabama, during a civil rights protest, and he sustained enthusiastic support for the cause throughout the decade. In 1963, a group of Conservative rabbis from Greenfield Park, New York, traveled to Birmingham to witness "in a testimony on behalf of the human rights and dignity of Negroes." Then, in 1965, Unitarian minister James J. Reeb of Boston was murdered while doing civil rights work in Selma.

Rabbi Arthur Hertzberg, leader of the Temple Emanu-El in Englewood, New Jersey, was unswerving in his dedication to racial equality, "telling his Conservative congregation in 1967, 'A vote for the Republican Party ... is a vote for racism, and I forbid it as an immoral act!'"[105]

"I have almost reached the regrettable conclusion that the Negro's great stumbling block in his stride towards freedom is not the White Citizen's Counciler or the Ku Klux Klanner, but the white moderate, who is more devoted to 'order' than justice."

~Martin Luther King, Jr.
Letter from Birmingham Jail

Chapter 8
Uncivil to disobedience

In Selma, Alabama, Martin Luther King, Jr., was joined by some 400 white clergy to march on behalf of voting rights in March of 1965. When the planned march from Selma to Montgomery was blocked by state troopers, King sent an appeal to clergy members nationwide to come to Selma on Tuesday, March 9. White ministers flew in from around the country to confront the racist government forces. Archbishop Iakovos, leader of the Greek Orthodox Church in North and South America and Rabbi Abraham Joshua Heschel, considered by many to be one of the most significant Jewish theologians of the 20th century, marched arm-in-arm with King as did Methodist Bishop John Wesley Lord. Bishop James Pike chartered a plane from San Francisco. Father Charles Carroll, of the St. Phillips Episcopal Church in San Jose, California made the trek, marching slowly with the aid of a heavy cane. Father Thomas Steensland, an Episcopal priest from Paso Robles walked heavily as well, having lost part of one foot to a land mine in World War II. Unitarian-Universalist ministers, most of them white, arrived en masse—perhaps one third of their total number in the U.S. traveled to Selma. They had particular impetus to march.

Unitarian-Univeralists Orloff Miller and Clark Olsen had responded to the aid request, together with James J. Reeb. Olsen said, "It was Turnback Tuesday, the day that Sheriff Clark's deputies and Mississippi State Troopers blocked the bridge to prevent the Selma to Montgomery march. Late in the day, King spoke at Brown's Chapel and suggested we all go eat dinner and return at 7 p.m. The three of us went to eat at what was normally a black cafe, though of course it was integrated that night. When we left we went the wrong way. About a half block down the street, near the Silver Moon Cafe, three men attacked us. One of them hit Jim across the side of the head with a club and he went down. Orloff dropped to the ground and covered his head where they proceeded to kick and punch him. I ran, but one of the three caught me and punched me and roughed me up before running off himself."

Olsen returned to his fallen companions where "Jim was babbling incoherently. We were afraid they would come back, so Orloff and I helped Jim stand and walked him around the block to an insurance business owned by a black family." An ambulance, black owned, in the shabby state of repair imposed by poverty, was summoned to transport Reeb to Birmingham. They were tailed by a carload of white men, one tire went flat, there was no radio, then a return to Selma riding on the rim, transfer to another ambulance and a state trooper who escorted them past the city limit. While Reeb was being treated, Olsen remembers, "Orloff and I were interviewed by Walter Cronkite, by Huntley-Brinkley, all the news media."

Reeb never regained consciousness and died on March 11. Johnson sent Air Force One to deliver Reeb's widow and father to Selma and sent a spray of yellow roses. The Board of Trustees of the Unitarian-Universalist Association, then meeting in Boston, adjourned to reconvene in Selma. King preached the sermon at Reeb's memorial service the following Monday, while Johnson took his Voting Rights Act to Congress—where it passed, earlier opposition falling away in the face of Reeb's violent demise. Olsen said he felt compelled to stay away from the memorial service. "I was the only witness who saw the man hit Jim," he told me. "I was concerned I might be targeted."

Among notable white ministers, Graham was conspicuous in his absence from those turbulent weeks in Selma as he was absent from every other civil rights march, rally or celebration over the years. He watched events unfold in Selma from Hawaii where he made bold statements but took no action. After King's death, Graham frequently described a much closer friendship with the assassinated leader than is apparent from the historical record or biographical material concerning King and those near to him. Graham's claim of intimacy appears to be based on the one occasion when King sermonized at a BGEA crusade and another when they were co-passengers on a flight to Argentina . In the late 1970s Graham told biographer Marshall Frady that King had said, "Billy, I realize that what I'm trying to do will never work until the heart is changed. That's why your work is so important." But Graham's assertion that King approved of his ministry and kid-glove handling of racial issues directly contradicts Kings public criticism of those like Graham who constantly placed law and order above concerns for civil liberties and whose support for integration was tepid, at best.

At the same time Graham told Frady, "I have to say though, that in time I became mixed up in my thinking about him. I became concerned about the people who were around him. I think it was because of Hoover, and all the things he kept warning me about in regard to King."[106]

This is Graham's only admission that he was anything but a great friend and admirer of King. Long after King and J. Edgar Hoover died, it would be revealed that FBI Chief Hoover had used wiretaps and bugging devices to keep careful tabs on King's political, social and sexual life. One can only guess what "all the things" whispered to Graham might have comprised.

Hoover's stories about wire-taps apparently fueled Graham's concern about the security of his own conversations. Near-paranoia emerged in an interview with biographer Marshall Frady when he said, "I'll have my crucifixion. I know that. It's going to come. I'm very frightened now by the high visibility of evangelicals in the country, and there are going to arise, in my judgement, a lot of false prophets, Elmer Gantrys, to take advantage of that, and I'll be included among them—it'll be some kind of frame-up. I can already sense hostility in areas that I never sensed it before. I am hated in some areas. Why, I even have to watch what I say on the telephone now. I even have to watch what I say to my wife at home. They've got this electronic equipment now, microphones that they could aim at you from some mountaintop around here five miles away and they could pick up absolutely everything you're saying in your own bedroom. I even have to watch what I say to my wife in our own bedroom now."[107]

Whatever his thinking, Graham failed to attend King's funeral five days after the murder, likely the largest such memorial service ever held in the United States. Over 200,000 people flooded Atlanta's streets. The crowd was replete with black celebrities from ministries, politics, entertainment and sports arenas. White attendees included: Vice President Hubert Humphrey; Senators Jacob Javits, Ted Kennedy, Gene McCarthy,

Charles Percy and Ralph Yarborough; Governors Nelson Rockefeller and George Romney; former Attorney General Bobby Kennedy and UAW Boss Walter Reuther.[108]

In his autobiography Graham said he learned of the assassination while golfing in Australia, where he was also conducting a crusade, and that his demanding schedule made attendance impossible. The Academy Awards and the start of the major league baseball season were both delayed in deference to the fallen leader.

Graham's frequent claims about King's approval of his stance on race are at odds with King's widely circulated exhortation from the Birmingham jail, in which he categorically condemned the position of clergymen who opposed civil disobedience, took them to task for obeying unjust laws, and spoke at eloquent length about the necessity for those of faith to demand change. He could have been directly rebutting Graham when he wrote, "You deplore the demonstrations taking place in Birmingham. But your statement, I am sorry to say, fails to express a similar concern for the conditions that brought about the demonstrations."

Further evidence of Graham's absence from the struggle for racial equality is found in the two thousand page history *Reporting Civil Rights: American Journalism 1941-1973* (Library of America, 2003). A collection of news stories by over 150 reporters from the movement's frontlines, written for local papers, national journals and major publishers, the two volume assemblage is stunning for its depth and scope. Graham is mentioned only once, in a negative reference to his preaching style, by David Halberstam. He was simply not a player on the civil rights stage.

King was operating in the tradition of Thoreau and other advocates of strategic civil disobedience, while Graham continually defended governments as instruments of God, and therefore to be obeyed, right or wrong.

In this regard it is worth noting that another Reverend King did find some use for Graham's work. Rev. Edwin King, a United Methodist minister, worked with the Mississippi Freedom Democratic Party in its voter registration and education campaigns and worked to integrate churches in Jackson. As reported by MLK biographer Taylor Branch, "On summer break in 1961, [Edwin] King had visited Lawson and other Freedom Riders imprisoned at Parchman Penitentiary, smuggling to them gift books by Gandhi concealed within Billy Graham jacket covers."[109]

In an unfortunate but typical lapse of scholarship, *Time* magazine's Graham apologists Nancy Gibbs and Michael Duffy asserted in *The Preacher and the Presidents* that it had been MLK who utilized the Graham covers in the Gandhi subterfuge.

Apropos of both Reverend Kings' embrace of civil disobedience, it's worth revisiting what historian Howard Zinn has noted concerning Thoreau's famed treatise on the subject, "At the center of Thoreau's great essay (though he doesn't make the reference) is that stunning idea expressed in the Declaration of Independence: governments are artificial creations, set up to serve the interests of the people. ...

"Thoreau has no respect for the law when the law allows war and protects slavery, nor for the justices of the Supreme Court, as they, obedient to the Constitution, affirm the legality of holding three million people as slaves.

"Thoreau's attitude toward law and toward the Constitution points very directly to the legal controversies of our own time, when certain Supreme Court justices and legal scholars insist their job is to decide what the Founding Fathers meant by the words they wrote in 1787. Thoreau asks why, in deciding moral questions, we must ask whether 'your grandfather, seventy years ago' entered into an agreement "to serve the devil" and therefore you must abide by that agreement, regardless of its human consequences."[110]

Graham explicitly disagreed. In his view, appeals like those of Thoreau or King to "higher law" stood subordinate to Biblical infallibility and Paul's letter to the Romans which posited that government is instituted by God and "is the servant of God to execute wrath on the wrongdoer" (Rom. 13:4).

Graham said, "I do believe we have the responsibility to obey the law. No matter what that law may be—it may be an unjust law—I believe we have a Christian responsibility to obey it. Otherwise you have anarchy."[111]

Throughout his career, Martin Luther King, Jr., continually grew in his understanding of the problems facing America. He started from race, but came to believe that the real issue was class, and so he took on labor organizing. Viewing the Vietnam war through the prism of class he saw that it was a rich man's war being fought by the poor, and he spoke out against it— losing the support of other civil rights leaders in the process. He had earned a huge amount of credibility in the Civil Rights struggle and was willing to spend that capital on less popular causes. He was unafraid to lead. Graham, on the other hand, spoke out strenuously against ministers who opposed the war, and it would be difficult to infer that he exempted King from his critique.

One of the things that doesn't ring true about Graham's repeated statements in recent years that he was a friend of "Mike's" (as King was known to intimates) and that King approved of his moderate approach, is the complete lack of understanding of King's evolution that Graham exhibited. Graham seemed to think that King died still espousing the narrow racial equality message he started from, whereas anyone who has even read a brief history of MLK's work, knows that his whole focus had shifted to matters of class, privilege, and empowerment. Graham kept him pigeonholed as an integrationist.

King's grasp of the social problems that underlay racism led to his strenuous opposition to the war. Blacks were greatly over-represented in the military and in casualties. He was well aware that whites and the wealthy were able to legally avoid the draft through college enrollment or helpful political connections, thus creating a de facto racial and social screen. In opposing the war, King sacrificed the support of some of his closest allies and divided the civil rights movement. Lyndon Johnson, a supporter of long standing, was just one of many who turned against him.

By contrast, Graham risked none of his popularity on anything even slightly controversial. He always found a ready excuse whether it was to disavow the previous night's sermon, as in Jackson, Mississippi, or ignore clerical pleas for help in Little Rock. One can only speculate on what impact Graham might have had on the civil rights issue if he had opted to act publicly on his professed belief in racial equality—if he had spoken in support of

King while King was alive. But without exception, Graham denounced racial upset and cast blame on outside agitators.

After a helicopter tour of Watts, in the aftermath of rioting in 1965, Graham announced that the rioters were "being exploited by a small, hard core of leftists," and called on Congress to pass "new tough laws ... to curb this kind of thing."[112]

"A tyrant must put on the appearance of uncommon devotion to religion. Subjects are less apprehensive of illegal treatment from a ruler whom they consider god-fearing and pious. On the other hand, they do less easily move against him, believing that he has the gods on his side."

~Aristotle

Chapter 9
Vietnam

Graham's alienation from the White House passed with Kennedy's assassination and he soon developed a close friendship with President Lyndon Johnson. He made frequent visits to the official mansion and later reported his participation with other administrative advisors in Presidential skinny-dipping in the White House pool—one of Johnson's preferred venues for policy discussions.

On the weekend before the 1964 Democratic Convention, Graham and his wife, Ruth, were dining with President Johnson and First Lady, Lady Bird in the White House. LBJ asked Graham for his recommendation for Vice President. According to Graham biographer John Pollock, "Under the table Ruth kicked her husband. Instead of taking the hint he said out loud, 'Why did you kick me?'" When pressed, she finally replied, "'Because you are supposed to limit your advice to the president to moral and spiritual issues.'"[113] Chastened, Graham waited until his wife had exited the room with the First Lady before answering LBJ: "Hubert Humphrey."

Johnson shared Graham's vehement anticommunist, antiunion sentiments, as did Herman and George Brown and Dan Root, owners of a public works construction company that had been the President's largest campaign funding source during his congressional career and stood poised to become larger still following a merger with Halliburton. Johnson had repeatedly used his influence to win the Brown brothers enormous federal contracts, to the point that some in Texas had taken to referring to him as the "Senator from Brown & Root." When the company teamed up with Johnson in 1937, it was a modestly successful Texas construction company, but by 1969 Brown & Root/Halliburton was number one in the country—thanks to military contracts linked to the war in Vietnam.

It is no surprise that Graham supported LBJ, a fellow Southern Baptist, over the Republican candidate, Barry Goldwater. Republicans hadn't become the nation's de facto religious party in 1964, and their candidate was openly critical of representatives of religion who sought political influence.

As Goldwater said on the floor of the Senate some years later, "I'm frankly sick and tired of the political preachers across this country telling me as a citizen that if I want to be a moral person, I must believe in A, B, C and D," he declared. "Just who do they think they are? And from where do they presume to claim the right to dictate their moral beliefs to me? And I am even more angry as a legislator who must endure the threats of every religious group who thinks it has some God-granted right to control my vote on every roll call in the Senate. I am warning them today: I will fight them every step of the way if they try to dictate their moral convictions to all Americans in the name of conservatism."[114]

Graham was perfectly clear where he stood on Vietnam. During 1965 he repeatedly warned about the global communist threat and insisted that the United States must maintain "the strongest military establishment on earth." Late that summer, speaking to the Denver Press Club he declared, "I have no sympathy for those clergymen who [urge] the U.S. to get out of Vietnam." Then, using an argument echoed by George Bush concerning his Iraq invasion four decades later, "Communism has to be stopped somewhere, whether it is in Hawaii or on the West Coast. The President believes it should be stopped in Vietnam."[115]

In a letter to Johnson, dated July 11, Graham wrote, "The Communists are moving fast toward their goal of world revolution. Perhaps God brought you to the kingdom for such an hour as this--to stop them. In doing so, you could be the man that helped save Christian civilization."[116]

At a prayer breakfast attended by Johnson and much of official Washington in 1966, Graham declared that Jesus was not an appeaser and told his audience, "Jesus said, 'Think not that I am come to send peace on earth: I came not to send peace but a sword.' There are those who have tried to reduce Christ to the level of a genial and innocuous appeaser; but Jesus said 'You are wrong—I have come as a fire-setter and a sword-wielder.'[117] 'I am come to send fire on the earth. ... Think not that I come to send peace on earth: I came not to send peace, but a sword.'"[118]

Graham's influence is nowhere more explicitly evident than when Johnson's plan for saturation bombing of Vietnam was accorded "the code name ROLLING THUNDER, taken from the theme hymn ['How Great Thou Art'] of the Billy Graham revival crusades."[119] Johnson needed validation for his Vietnam policies and in 1966 he decided that Graham should visit the troops at Christmas. Graham complied. He had written the president in glowing terms: "As God was with Washington at Valley Forge and with Lincoln in the darkest hours of the Civil War, so God will be with you."[120]

Graham, an occasional bear hunter, offered a curious story to his audience in Vietnam:

At Long Binh, he diverted the five thousand troops gathered to hear him with an anecdote about the man who had gone bear-hunting without a rifle and, after half an hour, came running out of the woods back toward the cabin where two companions were waiting: said Graham, his voice barraging over the loudspeakers with bumps of artillery in the distance, "They heard him hollering, 'Open that door! Open that door!' They looked out and saw a big bear chasing him. They opened the door, but just before he got there, the man stepped aside and the bear ran in. The man shut the door and shouted through the window, 'Skin that one, and I'll go get another!'" Beaming, Graham then cried to his grimed and helmeted congregation, "You might work that on Charlie sometime!"[121]

In 1967 Graham suggested that Johnson identify "those extremist groups who are teaching and advocating violence, training in guerilla tactics, and defying authority. ... The FBI and the President know who they are and what they are up to. Now the people need to know. Congress has no more urgent business than to pass laws with teeth in them."[122]

He repeated this allegation the following year, "guerilla war is now being planned by the anarchists."[123] He warned of impending terrorist operations to begin on Oct. 1.

Again, in late 1969, following the largest antiwar rally of the decade, he asserted that antiwar demonstrators were "radicals and those seeking to overthrow the American way of life."[123]

At every opportunity, Graham advocated continuation of the war. In 1968 he announced, "The stakes are much higher in Vietnam than anybody realizes. The stakes are extremely high for the Western world. Every American can be proud of the men in uniform who are representing our nation on that far-flung battle front. They are paying a great price for the victory they are almost certainly winning there."[124] Frye Gaillard reported in *The Progressive* that during television crusades "he would bring to the podium assorted young Marines, crewcut and earnest, to explain how God had helped them kill communists."[125]

Nor was Vietnam the only political issue on Graham's mind that year. In one of his frequent letters to Johnson, this one written June 21, 1968, he offered his counsel on the Supreme Court: "I just heard on the news that Chief Justice Warren has resigned. If this news proves to be correct, it is my prayer that you will give serious consideration to balancing the Court with a strong conservative as Chief Justice. I am convinced that many of the problems that have plagued America in the last few years are a direct result of some of the extreme rulings of the Court, especially in the field of criminology [sic]. I believe that our mutual friend, Governor John Connally would make an ideal and popular choice. He might not be popular with the extreme liberals and radicals who are already fighting you anyway but he would make a great Chief Justice."[126]

Later that summer the Democratic National Convention became the scene of one of the nodal episodes in a turbulent decade. Chicago police rioted, beating peaceful demonstrators on live TV, offering scenes that riveted the attention of audiences around the world. Middle-of-the-road Americans reacted viscerally to the excessive use of force broadcast live on TV.

Journalists for major news outlets were among those shoved, slammed, tear gassed and chased through the streets, some bloodied by police batons, and their reports flowed out into public awareness. Police excesses at other demonstrations across the country were questioned and challenged. Yet just a few months later, Graham informed a gathering of more than a thousand New York police officers that they were "God's agents for punishment."[127] Addressing the St. George Association, a New York organization comprised of Protestant policemen, Graham said "The Bible teaches us that the policeman is the agent of God." He continued, "And the authority that he has is given to him not only by the city and the state but ... by Almighty God. So you have a tremendous responsibility at this hour of revolution and anarchy and rebellion against all authority that is sweeping across our nation."[128]

After meeting with J. Edgar Hoover to receive a report on radical students he announced, "there is a small, highly organzied group of radicals" who were "determined to destroy what they call 'the system.'" Then, in an NBC-TV interview, he claimed to have inside knowledge that one hundred terrorist groups were preparing to destroy established order in the nation.[129]

"War is the statesman's game, the priest's delight, the lawyer's jest, the hired assassin's trade."

~Percy Bysshe Shelley

Chapter 10
Millions of little people

Graham's support for the war continued unabated while other religious leaders increasingly called for an end to U.S. involvement in Southeast Asia. In 1967, Martin Luther King spoke out against the war in a sermon at Riverside Church in New York City and Graham's response was that King's criticism "is an affront to the thousands of loyal Negro troops who are in Vietnam."[131]

At a Los Angeles press conference in spring, 1968, Graham was asked if he agreed with Episcopal Bishop James Pike's anti-draft position. "No, I don't agree with that." Then, specifically queried about Pike's recommendation for unconditional withdrawal from Vietnam, he replied, "No, I don't agree with him on that. I don't think any thinking person who has ever been to Asia could possibly agree to this unilateral action. I hope we have peace, but I hope we also remember that there are millions of little people in Asia that are scared to death that we are going to withdraw. They are depending on us to keep our word. They have put their lives on the line. Everything they have on the line."[132]

Unlike Graham, Pike had served in the military. Pike was a member of Naval intelligence during WWII, held a doctorate from Yale University and was a former lawyer for the Securities and Exchange Commission and instructor at George Washington University. Notwithstanding his controversial religious views, Pike was and is regarded by many as a leader in 20th Century Christian thought. Speaking before the Southern Baptist Convention Graham referred to anti-war clergymen and said, "Where many of these men get the 'Reverend' in front of their names, I do not know. Certainly they don't get it from God."[133]

In 1969 Graham returned to Madison Square Garden where the Rockefellers were once again major supporters, "David contributed, and Chase Manhattan Bank chairman George

Champion again helped lead the fundraising drive."[134] Nixon attended the New York crusade, and found his war efforts fully endorsed by Graham, who urged support for law and order and reminded attendees once again that the Bible specifically grants God's authority to government.

The Rockefellers undoubtedly understood that Graham was an advisor to Nixon on South American matters during this period. In explanation of his advisory position, Graham said, "'[Nixon] wanted to know what missionaries were thinking in certain countries because he felt that they knew more, many times, than the embassy knew about what was going on because they were much closer to the people.' Though Graham had left the board of the Wycliffe Bible Translators/Summer Institute of Linguistics, he maintained the political contacts his earlier involvement had spawned. "I meet the ambassadors, I meet the heads of state and I meet different people and talk to them,' said Graham, 'and sometimes they'll tell me things they'll never tell a visiting political leader—they'd never tell Kissinger, for example.'"[135]

In 1962 Graham had made two circuits of the southern continent starting with the oil giant, Venezuela, where he boated through Sun Oil Company's fields in Lake Maracaibo. Sunoco President J. Howard Pew, a financial backer of the Billy Graham Evangelistic Association, had personally arranged the tour. Graham met with state legislators in Maracaibo and toured under military guard.

In Colombia, his next stop, he met with a former president and renewed friendships with old contacts from the aviation ministries. Moving on to Ecuador, he met with other Wycliffe associates including widows of some of the missionaries whose death's Luce and Graham had made famous. From there he traveled to Peru and Chile, where he met with an evangelical named John Bolton, who Graham reported, "owned a lot of property." Next stop was Argentina, then in political turmoil. Former (and future) President Juan Peron was pulling strings from exile in Caracas, Venezuela, while the military and political parties grappled for power.

In the fall of that year, Graham went on a second South American tour beginning in Brazil, then Paraguay where he met with President Alfredo Stroessner, notorious for human rights abuses. From there he traveled to Argentina and Uruguay, continuing his crusade and meetings with whatever public officials he could engage.

Next came a return to Argentina where his visit coincided with the Cuban missile crisis. His sermon was laced with warnings about Communism and nuclear war. Graham met with members of the Argentinean cabinet including the defense minister who asked him to convey an offer of assistance, including use of two aircraft carriers, to Kennedy, "if it comes to war."

On his return to the U.S., Graham was summoned to brief Kennedy and Secretary of State Dean Rusk on his view of matters in South America, including the Argentinean offer.

U.S. involvement in post World War II Latin American affairs wobbled between covert and overt intervention, with fear of Castro's Cuban success as the principal impetus for government largesse and the lure of a resource-rich continent drawing international corporate players.

In 1961 Kennedy initiated the Alliance for Progress with a promise of $20 billion to bolster southern economies threatened by restive workers, then as now suffering huge disparities between enormous wealth and destitution. At the same time he signed off on the Bay of Pigs invasion without a significant military commitment, convinced by his military advisers that he could topple Castro on the cheap. Neither strategy yielded measurable success.

Lyndon Johnson sent a naval battle group to support the CIA-engineered coup in Brazil in 1964, an intervention which ushered in 20 years of military rule in South America's largest nation. Other U.S. meddling included the employment of Luis Echeverría Álvarez, president of Mexico from 1970-76. Alvarez was a CIA agent according to former CIA operative Philip Agee who also revealed CIA connections to President José Figueres Ferrer of Costa Rica. Ferrer held office in 1948-49, 1953-58 and again from 1970-74. Agee also stated that Alfonso López Michelsen, president of Colombia from 1974-78, was a CIA operative during his term of office.[136]

Kissinger was an adviser to Nelson Rockefeller, David Rockefeller, Johnson, Nixon and Ford, and returned as a consultant during both Bush presidencies. He advocated the 2003 invasion of Iraq and at this writing remains a staunch advocate for the occupation while arguing that it wasn't done properly. Kissinger's connection to war crimes and human rights violations include those committed as part of Chilean dictator Augusto Pinochet's Operation Condor. Condor was an international program of cooperation between military dictatorships throughout Latin America including Stroessner's Paraguay and Videla's Argentina. The conspiracy worked to assassinate Pinochet's enemies and to stage attacks in (at least) Argentina and Italy. Pinochet's agents also murdered Orlando Letelier, President Salvadore Allende's former foreign minister, and Letelier's Institute for Policy Studies colleague Ronni Moffitt in Washington D.C. in 1976. The CIA directly participated in Allende's overthrow and murder on 'Sept. 11, 1973, with Kissinger's full knowledge and support.[137]

In *The Sorrows of Empire* (Metropolitan Books, 2004), Chalmers Johnson reported, "Prosecutors in Chile, Argentina, Spain, and France would like to put former Secretary of State Henry Kissinger on trial for his support and sponsorship of the military dictatorships of Brazil, Chile, Uruguay, Paraguay, Bolivia, Argentina, and Ecuador while , in the 1970s, they were killing, torturing, and 'disappearing' their own citizens and those of neighboring lands."

At Nixon's behest, Kissinger steered Graham's below-the-radar ambassadorship around the globe. In September of 1969, Graham informed Nixon that he had scheduled an appointment for tea with Israeli Prime Minister Golda Meir and asked, "If you have any suggestions as to how I may contribute in this delicate Middle East situation, please let me know." Accompanying material in the National Archive indicates that Kissinger received a memo about this and was asked to phone Graham.[138]

When Nixon was planning his breakthrough visit to Red China in 1971, a memorandum from H.R. Haldeman to Kissinger noted that Billy Graham had been invited to visit Madam Chiang

Kai-shek and the generalissimo in Taipei. It read in part, "It is Graham's intention to try to explain things to them in whatever way we want them explained and also to meet with the missionaries in Formosa; among whom there is now a problem of strong resentment and anger towards the U.S. He views this as an opportunity to carry a private message of comfort from the President.

"The President has approved Graham's trip to Taipei and he therefore intends to go in early December." Haldeman then conveyed Nixon's instructions: "Would you please prepare a short briefing paper for Graham covering whatever background information he should have and whatever points you want him to make to the generalissimo.

"Graham wants to talk personally with the President before he goes also, but he should have your paper and suggestions before he does that." Kissinger prepared a six page paper titled "Recommended Talking Points."[139]

"Those who can make you believe absurdities can make you commit atrocities."

~Voltaire

Chapter 11
Bombing the dikes

In April, 1969, Graham sent a 13-page letter to Nixon titled, THE CONFIDENTIAL MISSIONARY PLAN FOR ENDING THE VIETNAM WAR. The missive included detailed plans for de-Americanizing the war, increasing propaganda and a recommendation to bomb North Vietnamese dikes. Graham wrote, "There are tens of thousands of North Vietnamese defectors in the south who could form the nucleus for both government and military operations. Why should all the fighting be in the south? Use North Vietnamese defectors to bomb and invade the north. Especially let them bomb the dikes which could over night destroy the economy of North Vietnam." In conclusion, he wrote, "The Communists are desperately afraid of a well armed South Vietnamese military power with an emphasis on guerilla warfare using Oriental methods. They look upon Americans as inferior. They look upon the other Vietnamese and Orientals as equals. ... Respectfully submitted, BG"[140]

The dikes are a massive complex of earthworks that both permit cultivation of Southeast Asia's principle staple, rice, and retain vast amounts of water. It was well understood by anyone familiar with the geography of the region, and underscored by Nixon's own estimate, that such bombing would kill a million people and wipe out an already poor nation's agricultural system.

The civilized world takes such matters very seriously. The German high commissioner in occupied Holland, Seyss-Inquart, was sentenced to death at Nuremberg for breaching dikes in Holland in World War II.

As explained by the Crimes of War Project ("a collaboration of journalists, lawyers and scholars dedicated to raising public awareness of the laws of war"): "First, it is forbidden to direct an attack against civilians who are not taking an active part in hostilities. Second, it is forbidden to attack civilian objects unless they make an effective contribution to your enemy's military operations. Thirdly, it is against the law to launch indiscriminate attacks — attacks that cannot be directed at a specific military target. Attacks are also considered indiscriminate if they violate the principle of proportionality. According to this important rule, the harm to civilians that is likely to be caused by an attack must not be excessive in relation to the concrete and direct military advantage that can be expected. Forces must also do everything feasible to minimize the likely harm caused to civilians by their military operations.

"Violations of these key principles of the laws of armed conflict are considered to be war crimes, for which individuals can potentially be held accountable."[141]

When the confidential missionaries plan "became available for public inspection in February 1989, Graham noted characteristically that the views contained in it were largely those of the missionaries and that he had merely conveyed those views to the President. It is clear, however, that he agreed with them, not only from his own statements in the report but also from the fact that six months after he had sent it to Nixon, he sent a copy to Henry Kissinger, assistant to the President for national security affairs, noting that Defense Secretary Melvin Laird had been impressed with it and expressing his hope that Kissinger would also pay heed to it."[142]

Graham's question, "Why should all the fighting be in the south?" surely fell on receptive ears. Not long after, Nixon moved the air war north and west.

Kissinger, recipient of Graham's dike-bombing scheme, received the 1973 Nobel Peace Prize—no small irony since he would later be sought for questioning in connection with war crimes investigations in Argentina, Brazil, Chile, France and Spain. In addition to Operation Condor, mentioned above, Kissinger would be directly accused of war crimes for the illegal bombing of Cambodia, complicity in assassination plots in Cyprus, Chile and the U.S. as well as endorsement and material support of genocide in East Timor.

In June 2004, linguist and political philosopher Noam Chomsky commented on what followed: "On May 27 [2004], *The New York Times* published one of the most incredible sentences

I've ever seen. They ran an article about the Nixon-Kissinger interchanges. Kissinger fought very hard through the courts to try to prevent it, but the courts permitted it. You read through it, and you see the following statement embedded in it. Nixon at one point informs Kissinger, his right-hand Eichmann, that he wanted bombing of Cambodia. And Kissinger loyally transmits the order to the Pentagon to carry out 'a massive bombing campaign in Cambodia. Anything that flies on anything that moves.' That is the most explicit call for what we call genocide when other people do it that I've ever seen in the historical record."[143]

Graham had specifically and repeatedly advocated a plan that amounted to genocide and his boosterism for U.S involvement was unflagging. He insisted in 1969 that, "There is no question—the war is already won militarily."[144] And he continued to condemn antiwar protesters for "giving comfort to the enemy."[145] This stance fit comfortably with his oft-reiterated position on obeisance to government. "I do believe we have the responsibility to obey the law. No matter what the law may be—it may be an unjust law—I believe we have a Christian responsibility to obey it."[146]

Privately, however, Graham was busy subverting the law to keep his Christian collaborators out of the service. Biographer William Martin reported, "When it became apparent that perhaps as many as four thousand unordained but 'full-time Christian workers,' including a sizable contingent from Bill Bright's Campus Crusade for Christ movement [which then as now was partially underwritten by BGEA], were about to be drafted in 1969, Graham placed an urgent call to the White House, contending that they should receive the same exemption granted to ordained ministers.

"In a memo to Haldeman and John Erlichman, Dwight Chapin reported that 'Dr. Graham states that ... on the President's Review Board there are one or two gentlemen who are antagonistic toward the work done by these Christian leaders ... Needless to say, Graham is very anxious to have someone look into this matter and to see that the policy of exempting these 'full-time Christian leaders' is carried through.' The White House obviously considered this as more than a minor annoyance to be finessed as gracefully as possible. Several staffers got involved in seeking a resolution, and one memo noted that 'since the board serves at the pleasure of the President, the most quiet and expeditious method of obtaining a review of this matter would be to replace at least some of its members.' Graham professed not to recall this episode, but the matter of deferring 'Billy Graham's people' was on the White House agenda for at least two months and a 'talking paper' for a telephone conversation with the evangelist directed that he be told there was 'little danger of a wholesale draft of these ministers.'"[147]

Billy Graham's private concern for Christian workers did not extend to his son, Franklin, insofar as he told the press, "I hope my son, who is nearing draft age, will gladly go and be willing to give his life."[148] Franklin may have been nearing draft age, but he had the safety net of white privilege and wealth as well as Graham's considerable influence to ensure that he would never actually be drafted.

When Franklin fell short on credits for high school graduation, his father intervened with the principal who said, "No problem, Dr. Graham."[149] Then Graham asked arms manufacturer Richard G. Tourneau (a.k.a. Le Tourneau) to dispense with entry rules and permit his unqualified son to enter Le Tourneau University, a religion-based technical college in Longview, Texas. Tourneau readily complied.

Tourneau, one of the businessmen Graham had cultivated during his Florida Bible Institute days, had a long history of contributing to Graham's enterprises, having bailed out a faltering Youth For Christ tour of Europe with a seven thousand dollar check in 1946 and continuing through the years.[150] Tourneau's Texas school trained mechanics and pilots for aviation ministries. In his autobiography, Franklin reported, "Le Tourneau was also designed to provide other tradesmen, such as welders and machinists, for R.G.'s factories, which were nearby. While I attended the school, some of those factories were manufacturing bomb casings for use in the Vietnam War."[151]

Tourneau's work included ousting native populations from the Amazon basin in cooperation with the Summer Institute of Linguistics. He established a 400,000 hectare ranch where his workers clear-cut rain forest and grazed cattle. "Although it emerged that profit was an objective, Le Tourneau said that the principal aim was the foundation of a Christian colony."[152] Tourneau invested as much as $8 million in the venture, named Tournavista. "Tournavista was to be a salesroom to demonstrate how Le Tourneau machines could demolish a hectare of forest in half an hour," but the machines "proved less economical than local labour." The project collapsed in 1964 when Tourneau conducted mass layoffs to forestall union organizing and civil unrest swept through the worker population. "Five years later the company asked the government to liquidate the holding."[153]

Like many another parent, Graham also helped his son find summer work by contacting likely employers. The first year, the summer of 1970, he called his friend Secretary of the Interior Walter Hickel to arrange a job in Hickel's home state of Alaska. The following summer it was a stint leading tour groups in the Mideast, using vehicles purchased by Billy Graham's organization. Next Franklin was hired to drive a new BGEA Land Rover from England to a mission in Mafraq, Jordan, and he dropped out of college for a semester to participate in the adventure. Toward the end of the following semester he was expelled from Le Tourneau for violation of school rules and was packed off to spend another summer in Jordan. He then attended a local Presbyterian junior college in Montreat and stuck with it until graduation in 1974. The Vietnam War had ended in the meantime, too soon for Franklin to "gladly go."

Billy Graham had avoided the army between his ministerial obligations and an undiagnosed illness that required convalescence in Florida instead of officer's training at Harvard, and now Franklin had also sidestepped military service despite a professed love of war.

By the time Franklin returned to college a year later "while Daddy was still in the frame of mind to pay the bills," he had been born again, married and fathered the first of four children. Having worked for BGEA and other evangelical operations in various capacities he decided to get a business degree instead of pursuing a religious education. He wrote, "No matter what my life's work, whether with my father in his crusades, leading Samaritan's Purse, or being involved in any other type of ministry, I needed to understand fundamental business principles."[154]

"'God's Plan' is often a front for men's plans and a cover for inadequacy, ignorance and evil."

~Mary Daly

Chapter 13
Domestic Intrigue

Graham, keenly attuned to politics by this point in his career, always professed innocence of political motives in the public arena. As he later admitted, "People took for granted that I was for Eisenhower, they took for granted that I was for Lyndon Johnson, they took for granted that I was for Nixon, and they were right, but I didn't endorse them openly in public."[155]

In fact, his friendship with both Johnson and Nixon led to one of his first assignments during the 1968 campaign when he was enlisted in Nixon's plan to weaken Johnson's support for Hubert Humphrey. Vice President Humphrey was cut from wholly different cloth than Johnson, whose support for Humphrey's presidential bid was quiescent at best.

Humphrey, known as "the happy warrior," was a populist-leaning liberal, solidly supportive of labor, social welfare programs and civil rights. His image was that of a humanitarian idealist determined to fight the good fight, as versus Johnson's well-earned reputation as a back room pol—an arm-twister willing, even eager, to punch below the belt. A Minnesotan, Humphrey's enlistment as Johnson's vice presidential running mate had been driven by the need for geographic balance on the ticket and his nomination as the Democrats' 1968 standard bearer was by default. Robert Kennedy had been the odds-on favorite to win the nomination that summer until he was gunned down in a Los Angeles hotel. Kennedy's surging popularity and the combined debacles of Vietnam and the racial and social upheaval at home had driven Johnson to withdraw from the race. Humphrey, who enjoyed a reputation for creative compromise and considerable visibility as the sitting vice president, stepped in as the standard-bearer for a bitterly divided and embattled party in a bitterly divided nation.

As reported by historian Stanley Kutler, Nixon "met Billy Graham in Pittsburgh on September 8 [1968] and asked him to deliver a confidential message to the President. Nixon passed the word that he would never embarrass the President after the election, that he would continually seek his advice, and that he would ask Johnson to undertake special missions to foreign countries. He assured the President that when the Vietnam war was settled, he would give Johnson a major share of credit and do everything to ensure the President's place in history. A week later Graham delivered the message and recorded that the President warmly appreciated and was 'touched' by Nixon's gesture. His last words were that he intended 'to loyally support' Humphrey, but if Nixon was elected he would "do all in my power to cooperate with him.' ... So Johnson deserted Humphrey, whom he often professed to love and admire."[156]

Nixon never delivered on his promises to LBJ, immediately relegated him to the sidelines, blamed war failures on his predecessor and later gave Kissinger credit for achieving peace.

Throughout the Nixon presidency Graham remained a central player. Historian John Prados, intimately familiar with the Nixon White House tapes, noted, "At the time of Nixon's invasion of Cambodia at the end of April 1970, Billy Graham was among those persons whom the president consulted by telephone, stiffening Nixon's resolve for an action accurately expected to be inflammatory."[157]

At Kent State University, the Cambodian bombing stirred student demonstrations that resulted in the murder of four of their number by National Guard troops. Shortly thereafter, Graham invited Nixon to address his Knoxville crusade, held on the campus of the University of Tennessee while parents of Kent State students were still burying the dead. This was to be the President's first campus appearance following the Cambodian incursion, three weeks earlier. It was also the first time a sitting president had addressed a mass evangelistic meeting and he arrived with First Lady Pat Nixon, Henry Kissinger and Congressman Bill Brock, the Republican candidate for Al Gore, Sr.'s U.S. Senate seat, in tow.

In his glowing introduction, Graham intoned, "All Americans may not agree with the decision a president makes— but he is our president ..."[158]

Retired atmospheric scientist Gary Briggs, now of Weaverville, N.C., recalled: " I attended the Billy Graham crusade in Knoxville the day president Richard Nixon was invited to speak. Ironically, Nixon's speech was not blatantly war mongering and did not impress me or ruffle my feathers. But Graham's introduction to Nixon did. He called Nixon very courageous to order an expansion of that war into Cambodia."

While Nixon spoke, police were quelling an antiwar protest in the hall with the aid of the UT football team, arresting protest leaders and hauling them out of the stadium.

During his Euro '70 crusade, which made use of the latest TV technology to enable translated simulcasts throughout Europe of the Dortmund, Germany event, Graham fended off widespread objections to his perceived endorsement of the war. He soothed his German detractors at a pre-crusade meeting of ministers by claiming to represent "the Kingdom of God ... My flag is the flag of Christ. Why did Jesus Christ not lead a demonstration against the tyranny of Rome? Why did Paul not lead a demonstration? Because they represented a different Kingdom."

He then neatly turned the argument back on the Germans by playing the Hitler card. "I cannot defend the United States, any more than you can defend what went on in the '30s and '40s in Germany." And with a stage magician's sleight-of-hand he turned that card into a winning hand by adding, "Now concerning Vietnam, I promise you this. If Germany is invaded by a foreign power, and the U.S. comes to your aid, I will not lead a demonstration down Pennsylvania Avenue against giving you that aid."[159]

It was a clever, if disingenuous finesse—equating the U.S. intervention in Vietnam's civil war with repulsion of a foreign invasion of Europe. Although the statement was reportedly accorded "prolonged and unanimous applause" from the German clergy, Graham had taken the precaution of ordering construction of a speaker's platform high enough that the cameras wouldn't show antiwar protesters, should they arrive at the crusade, as well as a soundproof broadcast booth for use in the event that antiwar demonstrations became embarrassingly loud.[160]

In the midst of rising antiwar sentiment in the U.S., Graham, Hobart Lewis (president of *Reader's Digest*), entertainer Bob Hope and hotelier J. Willard Marriott organized "Honor America Day" at Nixon's behest. The Washington, D.C. rally, staged by Disney and held on July 4, 1970, was billed as a nonpartisan event, but its advocacy was thinly disguised. Hope had been an outspoken advocate for Nixon's policies, both foreign and domestic, and Lewis had steered his magazine's support for Nixon since the 1950s. Organizers staged a march that was openly pro-war and were confronted by angry antiwar demonstrators. A report in the Billy Graham Evangelistic Association Archives notes, "Graham's role included serving as one of a number of directors of the event, at which he was the featured speaker."[161]

The event was closely coordinated with Gordon C. Strachan, an assistant to Herbert G. Klein, Director of Communications for the Executive Branch. Strachan worked primarily under the supervision of Jeb S. Magruder, deputy director of communications, who reported directly to Klein and White House Chief of Staff H. R. Haldeman.[162] BGEA personnel including Cliff Barrows and Walter Smyth worked full-time on the project and Graham touted it on his *Hour of Decision* broadcast.

In response to this and other endorsements of the war, Graham drew increasing criticism from within Christian circles. Fellow clergymen publicly questioned his stance, "including the Reverend Ernest Campbell of New York's Riverside Church, who preached a sermon entitled 'An Open Letter to Billy Graham,' in which he implored the evangelist to use his influence with Nixon to try to stop the bombing."[163]

Instead, Graham used his influence with Nixon for his own purposes. In 1971, Graham's organization was given a hard look by the Internal Revenue Service and he took his troubles to Nixon. An Oval Office tape recorded the president's comments to Chief of Staff Haldeman on September thirteenth of that year. "Billy Graham tells an astonishing thing. The IRS is battering the shit out of him. Some sonofabitch came to him and gave him a three-hour grilling about how much he, you know, how much his contribution is worth and he told it to [John] Connally. Well, Connally took the name of the guy. I just got to get that nailed down to Connally when you get back. He didn't know it. Now here's the point. Bob, *please* get me the names of the Jews, you know, the big Jewish contributors of the Democrats ... All right. Could we please investigate some of the cocksuckers? That's all.

"Now, look at here. Here IRS is going after Billy Graham tooth and nail. Are they going after Eugene Carson Blake [President of the National Council of Churches, a liberal group]? I asked—you know, what I mean is, Goddamn. I don't believe—I just don't know whether we are being as rough about it. That's all."[164]

Whatever administration action followed this conversation, Graham's problem was apparently resolved. The preacher sent Nixon a hand-written note on December 10: "My expectations were high when you took office nearly two years ago, but you have exceeded [them] in every way! You have given moral and spiritual leadership to the nation at a time when we desperately need it—in addition to courageous political leadership! Thank you!"[165]

During the 1972 campaign, Graham worked unabashedly for Nixon's reelection, albeit behind the scenes. The Richard M. Nixon Presidential Materials in the National Archive contain numerous weekly talking points memos for Graham's meetings with Haldeman pertaining to the campaign. In a memo to Bob Haldeman dated Feb. 8, 1971, Nixon wrote, "Some time ago I pointed up the importance of unmasking [Edwin] Muskie's moderate image and I urged that this particularly be done in the South." Haldeman noted, "In talking to Billy Graham Sunday he came at this point very strongly and said that Muskie was becoming increasingly acceptable in the South because most southerners thought that he was a moderate, both domestically and in the field of foreign policy."[166]

Entries in Haldeman's diary as well as a memo from Haldeman aide Lawrence M. Higby to Haldeman titled "Alsop use of Graham Report of LBJ/McGovern Meeting," dated Aug.

28, 1972. "As I indicated to you earlier, John Ehrlichman [Assistant to the President for Domestic Affairs] called suggesting that we get the Billy Graham report on the McGovern/LBJ meeting to Alsop for use in his column. John thought that if you agreed this was a good idea, that you should proceed with making whatever arrangements necessary."[167]

McGovern had called on Johnson to request that the President make campaign appearances on his behalf. Graham is seen here using his personal friendship and contact with Johnson to supply information to the Nixon campaign. Conservative columnist Stewart Alsop was evidently the intended recipient of Graham's campaign intelligence. There is no direct mention of the meeting in any of Alsop's regular *Newsweek* columns leading up to the November election, but the accuracy of Haldeman's diary would be established once again when the Nixon library released documents in 2007.

"In times of universal deceit, telling the truth will be a revolutionary act."

~George Orwell

Chapter 13
Curious Conversations

Billy Graham's voice on the tape is quite distinct. "This stranglehold has got to be broken or this country's going down the drain." Graham was talking with Richard Nixon about alleged Jewish control over the news media in the United States. There was nothing unusual about the setting, but this 1972 visit was recorded by a president whose infamous tapes are now scrutinized by legions of curious historians. Hence, thirty years after the words left the good Christian's mouth, he was forced to defend them when the Associated Press broke the story. He told the AP:

> *Although I have no memory of the occasion, I deeply regret comments I apparently made in an Oval Office conversation with President Nixon . . . some 30 years ago,"* Graham said in a statement released by his Texas public relations firm. *"They do not reflect my views, and I sincerely apologize for any offense caused by the remarks.*
> —AP wire story, March 2, 2002

For the most part and in most places, Graham was given a pass on this statement, including a much publicized meeting with Jewish leaders who accepted his dissembling mea culpa. The Asheville Citizen-Times, Graham's hometown daily, editorialized, "taken in the context of his life's work ... and recent apology ... Graham appears to have stepped away from that pact."[168]

The "pact" was sealed in the next sentences of that same conversation.

> *"You believe that?" Nixon said in response.*
> *"Yes, sir," Graham said.*
> *"Oh boy. So do I," Nixon agreed, then said: "I can't ever say that, but I believe it."*

> *"No, but if you get elected a second time, then*
> *we might be able to do something," Graham said,*
> *reassuring the president.*
> —*AP wire story, March 2, 2002*

Newspaper and broadcast reports about Graham's comments, condensed in the way all such reporting must be, tended to give the impression that the exchange was brief. Transcripts of the conversation, however, reveal that the discussion rarely strayed from that topic for over an hour and a half. Graham's comments included: "They're the ones putting out the pornographic stuff;" and "They are undermining the country." Nor is the record complete—about twenty minutes of the recording, in two segments, was excised before public access was granted.[169]

Further on in the conversation Graham says, "A lot of the Jews are great friends of mine. They swarm around me and are friendly to me. Because they know I am friendly to Israel and so forth. They don't know how I really feel about what they're doing to this country."

Nixon responds, "You must not let them know."

After Graham departs, Nixon tells Haldeman, "You know it was good we got this point about the Jews across."

His Chief of Staff responds, "It's a shocking point."

Nixon concludes, "Well, it's also the Jews are [an] irreligious, atheistic, immoral bunch of bastards."[170]

Nor did Graham's involvement in that conversation end when he exited the White House. He wrote a follow-up letter in which he promised, "I will try to follow through faithfully on each point we discussed."[171] Graham's blatant bigotry at the time of these utterances is irrefutable, though many have come to his defense by citing his public record of support for Israel—a position which is far more political than religious. His defense thirty years later bears closer scrutiny. What are we to make of a preacher who insists that his words don't reflect his beliefs?

Nixon wasn't the only person in his White House who maintained records. H.R. Haldeman, Nixon's chief of staff from his inauguration in 1969 until shortly before the president's resignation, kept a daily diary which was published in 1994, a year after Haldeman's death. The Chief of Staff noted a conversation between Nixon and Graham on Feb. 1, 1972 about "the terrible problem arising from the total Jewish domination of the media, and agreement that this was something that would have to be dealt with."[172] Haldeman quoted Graham as saying, "the Bible says there are satanic Jews, and that's where our problem arises."[173] Though this statement doesn't occur on the tape, scholars have surmised it may have been said in the redacted portions of the recording.

The tapes corroborate the overall accuracy of Haldeman's diary, but Graham claimed in a *Life* magazine interview, Nov. 2, 1994. "I never discussed the Jewish people, the Jewish problem, or if there is a problem, with the President, ever. If I participated in any such conversation, I would have been very pro-Jewish because I've been that way ever since I can remember."[174]

Referring to Graham's veracity in other matters, John Minder, Dean of Florida Bible Institute while Graham was a student there, said, "Billy has a way of making the story better over the years. He starts remembering it the way he'd like it to have been, which isn't always the way it necessarily was, y'know."[175]

Haldeman's account is elsewhere replete with detailed descriptions of Graham's involvement in politics. During the 1972 election, Nixon was understandably concerned that George Wallace might make another run for office, despite the would-be assassin's bullet that had left him paraplegic. The Republican "southern strategy" required support from the racist whites who comprised Wallace's most ardent followers. White House operatives decided that Graham should be enlisted to talk Gov. George Wallace out of entering the presidential race (as an independent) because "Graham has a line to Wallace through Mrs. Wallace, who has become a Christian."[176]

Graham accepted the assignment and, on July 18, shortly after the former governor was wheeled out of his latest surgery to address a festering bullet wound, the minister reached him by phone. The next day Graham reported to Nixon, "Wallace had assured him there was almost no chance that he would run. He did ask Graham whether he would take more votes from Nixon or [Democratic candidate George] McGovern if he did run; Graham replied that three out of four Wallace voters would otherwise go to Nixon. Wallace swore that he would never turn one hand to help McGovern."[177]

Wallace had achieved national fame as the Alabama governor who stood up forcefully against integration. In his inaugural speech he declared, "I say segregation now, segregation tomorrow, segregation forever." He personally blocked the door at the University of Alabama to prevent entry of black students and ordered state police to block Martin Luther King's march from Selma. His independent run for the presidency in 1968 had almost cost Nixon the White House, since Wallace peeled away southern support in a narrowly contested election. In 1972 he defeated McGovern in the Florida primary and enjoyed strong support nationwide. While campaigning in Maryland, in May of that year, Wallace was shot five times by a would-be assassin.

McGovern, running as an anti-war candidate, was the antithesis of the white supremacist Wallace who sneered at northerners and "pointy-headed intellectuals." A soft-spoken liberal from South Dakota, McGovern was professorial, thoughtful and engaged in an issues-based race for the White House. Nixon, co-author of the Republican "southern strategy," was busily using race as an issue to end the Democrats' century-long domination of politics below the Mason-Dixon line. Whereas the Wallace candidacy had given racist and conservative Democrats an opportunity to cast votes against the party's liberal national candidates in the 1968 general election and in 1972 primaries, Nixon operatives were eager to draw those same voters into the Republican camp.

In the topsy-turvy world of presidential politics, Nixon had run as a peace candidate against Humphrey, whom he pasted with responsibility for Johnson's unpopular war policies. As author Christopher Hitchens (*The Trial of Henry Kissinger*, Verso, 2002) and others have documented, during that campaign, Nixon's operatives including Kissinger ensured failure of Johnson's peace talks by promising South Vietnamese leaders that they would get a better deal under a Republican administration. The south boycotted talks until after the election.

Publicly, Nixon promised the nation he had a recipe to end the conflict in Vietnam, and, after his narrow win, immediately escalated the war. In 1972, facing an explicitly anti-war opponent, Nixon stressed the importance of maintaining a stable leadership during wartime, touted ongoing peace talks, and quietly played on southern racism. Despite discovery that summer of the Watergate break-in, the first in a series of criminal acts which would bury his presidency less than two years later, Nixon was well on his way to an electoral landslide when he dispatched Graham to defuse a possible Wallace challenge for southern votes.

The timing of Graham's phone call seems, at best, tasteless. It wouldn't be unreasonable to expect that a ministerial check-in after serious surgery had more to do with matters of the spirit than of the body politic. Haldeman says Graham reported, "... he asked Graham to come and see him and asked him in the meantime to pray for him and indicated that he's concerned because his abscess won't heal."[178]

Wallace was a paraplegic suffering from the lingering effects of an assassination attempt, asking for Graham's intercession with God in the hours after yet another surgery. Graham nevertheless forged ahead with his political hatchet job.

Graham gave Haldeman "names of all his Christian youth types." and it was noted, "He's very enthusiastic and thinks we have a very good group to work with us. He also feels we have a good chance on the blacks by splitting them and getting the religious blacks who are scared of the criminal elements and so on to come over to our side. He thinks we're in good shape with the Jews."[179]

As noted in an interview published in *Life* magazine in 1994: "Graham further acknowledges that he brought black leaders to the White House—but not, as Haldeman says, in hopes of 'splitting' them, but simply to 'better the relationship between Nixon and the black community.' This is hard for the visitor to swallow. Didn't Graham hope to help Nixon politically? He pauses before answering and then says quietly, 'I suppose that would have been true.'"[180]

In July, 2007, the Nixon Library and Archives released documents from that period which provide further insight into Graham's efforts. In a memo dated December 30, 1969, Nixon instructed White House Chief of Staff H.R. Haldeman to "follow up with Billy Graham in his work with Negro ministers across the country. He feels this is our best chance to make inroads into the Negro community. I am inclined to agree with him."[181]

Following up, Haldeman wrote a note to his assistant, Leonard Garment, on January 16, 1970. " The President is extremely interested in following up with Billy Graham in the work he is doing with Negro ministers across the country. He feels, as does Graham. that this may be our best chance to make inroads into the Negro community. I understand you've been in touch with Reverend Graham on this matter, particularly in relation to Reverend Edward Hill. In light of the President's continual interest in this project, would you please proceed to meet directly with Dr. Graham and provide the President with a status report of how we are proceeding with this project and what our future plans are."[182]

"Religion is a monumental chapter in the history of human egotism."

~William James

Chapter 14
Secure briefings

Not long after the 1972 election, Graham visited India and Iran at Nixon's behest and reported back on his talks with Prime Minister Indira Gandhi and the Shah. The unofficial ambassador's letters were included in a National Security Council briefing prepared by Henry Kissinger, Dec. 6, 1972.

Graham's letter concerning the Indian Prime Minister Gandhi read in part: "She said some of her people, especially the opposition, were convinced of CIA involvement in border incidents. I got the impression that she did not personally believe these allegations, but that her opposition was putting pressure on her. I told her that I was certain that this was not true. I stated that I had checked in very carefully with responsible State Department people and they had told me these allegations were false. She seemed to accept my assurance."[183]

Agee as well as other insiders and investigators would eventually establish that Graham was completely wrong in this assertion. Pakistan had lost half its territory to India in a 1970 war and border incidents continued. CIA complicity in the region's warring and political machinations was probably well known to Gandhi. The U.S. spy organization worked closely with ISI (Inter-Services Intelligence), Pakistan's secret police and security organization, for decades and Kissinger used contacts in the Pakistani government in his secret dealings with China.

In the letter to Kissinger, Graham went on to discuss Gandhi's concern that Americans wrongly perceived India to be an ally of the USSR. He said she found common ground with the USSR because of their shared problems with China, and had communicated her hope that a new U.S. ambassador would be "a man of great prestige in America, and a person who had a knowledge and a sensitivity about India."[184] Further on Graham inserted his own suggestion concerning appropriate diplomatic behavior for the Prime Minister: "I also got the impression that she would welcome any advance that you might personally make. In my personal judgment, she should show some advancing too. For a starter she might get over to the Indian people their great debt to America!" Nixon underlined the final sentence and scrawled "Right. MacGruder note!"[185] Such arrogant and condescending remarks surely fell on receptive ears. As Kissinger and other Nixon intimates have reported, Nixon detested Gandhi and routinely referred to her as "that bitch."

Kissinger's cover notes to Nixon included a synopsis of Graham's conversation with Iran's dictator. "He also had a good talk with the Shah whom he found very happy over your reelection. The Shah said that your reelection had 'probably saved Western civilization' and he is clearly looking forward to the day when peace is achieved in Vietnam and you can turn more of your attention to other pressing world problems."[186]

In the accompanying letter Graham wrote "First: He said if I was President Nixon I would put more young men in my cabinet.

"Second: He said, 'I was a hawk three years ago on Vietnam but the reasons for staying in Vietnam no longer exist.' ... He said that it was very imperative for you to get out of Vietnam now. He said it would make you the world leader and the world desperately needs a leader of your caliber."[187]

Then he added, "We had a rather lengthy discussion of spiritual things. I reminded him that Daniel the Prophet was the First Prime Minister of Persia under Cyrus—whose elevation to power the Shah had celebrated a few months ago. I reminded him of an obscure prophecy by Jeremiah the Prophet that says, 'That it shall come to pass in the latter days I will bring again the captivity of Persia, saith the Lord.' This prophecy indicates that there would come a time when Persia would rise again as a major power. I suggested the possibility of the beginnings of Persia's rise was now taking place under the leadership of His Majesty."[188] Numerous lines including "young men," "get out of Vietnam," and "you have already proven you are not a coward," in Graham's Shah letter were underlined in Nixon's heavy hand, with notes directed to the attention of both Haldeman and Ehrlichman.

The Shah's rise in power that Graham lauded in this letter had been engineered by the CIA. In 1951 the Iranian parliament had nationalized the country's oil industry, giving the boot to the Anglo-Iranian Oil Company (later renamed British Petroleum), which had enjoyed a monopoly under the Shah. The U.S. and Britain planned and executed a coup d'etat of sorts in 1953, tossing aside the popularly elected government and returning the Shah to more or less dictatorial power and the oil trade to Western hands. Though the rationale offered for the coup was restoration of constitutional rule, the Shah regarded himself as heir to the kings of ancient Iran. By the 1960s he was the preeminent leader in the Mideast, the self-styled "Guardian" of the Persian Gulf and a powerful ally of Egypt, Jordan, Morocco, Saudi Arabia and other Arab states. Though he stressed literacy and granted women the right to vote, he simultaneously moved the country to one-party rule with the help of a repressive national police force.

In January, 1973, Graham issued a revisionist version of his record on the Vietnam war in the form of a widely circulated press release. He claimed to have been criticized by "both hawks and doves for my position ..." and took shelter in the Bible which he reiterated, "would indicate that we will always have wars on earth until the coming of the Prince of Peace." He then stated unequivocally, "I have never advocated war. I deplore it!"[189]

Graham's defense of the war took him into unusual philosophic territory. "Graham was asked by *Newsweek* magazine in 1973 how he felt about President Nixon's resumption of bombing North Vietnam. He responded that the world has a lot of violence that doesn't make headlines, there are many being killed by drunken drivers and crime. 'But what of the bombing?' persisted *Newsweek*. Graham said he deplored the suffering and killing in the war and prayed that it could be ended as soon as possible. 'But we also have to realize that there are hundreds of thousands of deaths attributed to smoking.'"[190] *The New York Times* reported that he also likened the bombing to drinking, saying, "A thousand people are killed every week on the American highways, and half of those are attributed to alcohol. Where are the demonstrations against alcohol?"[191]

The Watergate break-in had been discovered in the summer of 1972 and a direct connection to Nixon's Committee to Reelect the President was first reported in the *Washington Post* on August 4, though it wouldn't gain traction until after Nixon's landslide victory over George McGovern. Graham was in weekly contact with the White House.

On July 11, 2007—when the Nixon Presidential Library passed from control by private backers to the U.S. National Archives—the library released 78,000 pages of previously secret documents, along with 11-and-a-half hours of recordings. Among the memos were several connecting Graham to the campaign, including a report on a White House meeting between McGovern and Johnson which Nixon's campaign passed on to columnist Stewart Alsop in September of that year. Alsop all but endorsed Nixon in his weekly *Newsweek* column, in which he repeatedly shredded McGovern's character, but there is no direct reference to the meeting in any of of the writer's columns that fall.

One of the newly released tapes is of a phone call on Nov. 3, 1972—four days before the election—in which White House Special Counsel Chuck Colson gave Nixon a detailed status report on numerous campaign issues. "Billy Graham's thing has moved very well—his statement supporting us, supporting you, on the integrity and on the morality issue," Colson told the president. "He came through very well."[192]

George Washington University maintains a collection related to the National Security Archives and recorded an interview with John Ehrlichman on February 7, 1999. Ehrlichman was a member of Nixon's inner circle and had worked for him since his 1960 presidential run. He was convicted of conspiracy, obstruction of justice, perjury and other charges related to Watergate on January 1, 1975 and served eighteen months in prison.

The interviewer asked Ehrlichman, "How important was a man like Billy Graham to Nixon?"

Ehrlichman replied: "Billy Graham was a very important figure to Richard Nixon, as he has been to Lyndon Johnson, and some other people in government. I'm not so sure that Nixon took Billy Graham to heart. I think it was much more a cerebral thing, than it was a spiritual or a soul thing. I think from time to time Reverend Graham gave him advice - I'm not so sure that he, Nixon, accepted the advice. They were in frequent contact, and Billy Graham was a good influence on some of the rest of us - whether he was on Richard Nixon or not."

The interviewer mentioned Nixon's appearance at the Knoxville crusade and asked, "How important at that time was public manifestation of support to ...."

Ehrichman cut him off and said: "Oh I think very important - I think there's an element in this country who vested great confidence in anybody who was Billy Graham's friend, Billy Graham's ally, who took part in Billy Graham's programs. there's a, there's a kind of a very conservative religious center of gravity in this country, that was very much appealed to by that connection."

By spring of 1973 the news for the administration was almost all bad.

Graham remained upbeat however and continued his public relations campaign for the President. A memorandum to Nixon from Presidential Secretary Lawrence M. Higby recorded one such effort on May 2, 1973. "Billy Graham called you early this morning -- I took the call. He wanted to pass on two things. First, that you read the attached transcript done by Mr. [Louis] Nizer this morning on the CBS morning news. He feels that people are finally starting to realize that this whole Watergate situation is overblown and unfair and that Nizer does a good job of stating this.

"Secondly, he wanted to pass on to you his suggestion that wherever possible we create picture situations such as the one yesterday with you and [German Chancellor] Willy Brandt. This causes public focus on the fact that the President is not bogged down on one issue, but is working in other areas. He feels the more of this type of thing we can do, the better." Then Higby quoted Graham, "The American people need to be diverted from Watergate and pictures such as the one yesterday with you and Brandt do this ..."[193]

As investigation of the Watergate break-in and subsequent cover-up and obstruction of justice spiraled in toward

Nixon, Graham continued his public and private support. When Nixon's guilt was clearly established, Graham claims he was devastated when he learned that Nixon had deceived him. He had attested to Nixon's high moral character, repeatedly and publicly for years, assuring voters that Nixon could be trusted. Was he rocked by personal betrayal or the public exposure of his own error?

When the word "secularism" was mysteriously changed to "socialism" in the pamphlet distributed in Britian, he had blamed the home office. When his anti-Catholic machinations blew up, he had blamed Norman Vincent Peale. When CIA funding of his South American crusades came to light, he had claimed no knowledge. Concerning Nixon, what was going to be his excuse?

"I was born a heretic. I distrust those people who know so well what God wants them to do, because I notice it always coincides with their own desire."

~**Susan B. Anthony**

Chapter 15
Disavowal

Over the years, as Graham explained and re-explained his close friendship with Nixon, he continued to condemn the taped foul language—alledgedly never used in Graham's presence—while giving his friend a pass on all of his very real crimes: conspiracy to burglarize, bribe, extort, subvert justice and the rest. He eventually shifted the blame away from the President by suggesting, "I think it was sleeping pills. Sleeping pills and demons. I think there was definitely some demon power involved."[194]

He was asked about Nixon by *Time* magazine, in 1990, "Did he express any regret about Watergate?" Graham replied, "Oh, he apologized about the language. He said, 'There are many words that I used that I never knew before.'"[195] Graham's naiveté or spin in relating this putative quote evades *Time*'s question concerning repentance but suggests the question—how could Nixon rationally claim to have used vernacular he didn't know?

Supportive friendship is a two way street, and friendship with a President partakes of considerable power. Haldeman's diary notes that when Graham ran into trouble with the IRS, the preacher turned to Nixon for help. "Yes, he concedes, Haldeman is right—Graham once informed the President that he was being audited by the IRS. But he stresses, 'I certainly didn't bring it up with any thought that [he] would do anything about it. I think it was perfectly in order, in a general conversation, to make a remark that I'm being audited."[196]

In widely reported public statements, Graham dissembled when pressed about his relationship with Nixon saying, "I'm just a personal friend. That's all. In no way would he ask me military strategy. He's never even discussed it with me. If I have something to say to President Nixon, I'll do it privately and I won't announce it from the rooftops with a lot of publicity."[197]

Yet his private interventions were reported by others. In a sermon which questioned Graham's apology for his anti-Jewish plotting with Nixon, Rabbi Samuel M. Stahl credited the minister as a friend of Israel. "In a recent Letter to the Editor of *The New York Times,* Georgette Bennett, [Rabbi Marc H.] Tanenbaum's widow, recalled a marvelous story her husband told her about Graham's intervention in the 1973 war in Israel. Many others had also intervened. Yet it was only after Graham's phone call to Nixon that the president sent a military airlift to Israel. It was that dramatic action that helped to insure Israel's survival."[198] Tanenbaum was an internationally active figure, with wide connections in government, ecumenicism and peace activism who could easily have been in a position to learn of such an intervention.

Little did Graham suspect that the most thoroughly documented presidency in history would prove him false over and over again. Between tapes, memos and diaries it later became known that Nixon and Haldeman gave Graham weekly or biweekly updates on every issue that might concern his audience[199], that they had given him talking points to enable him to combat McGovern's support among antiwar religious groups[190] and that Graham had been viewed and discussed as a useful tool rather than simply a personal friend.[201]

Six days before the signing of the Paris truce agreement, in January 1973, Graham told *The New York Times* "he had 'doubted from the beginning' the wisdom of 'sending American troops anywhere without the will to win ... we entered the war almost deliberately to lose it ... I don't think we should ever fight these long-drawn-out, halfhearted wars. It's like cutting a cat's tail off a half-inch at a time.'"[202] Soon thereafter, the president's appointment secretary Dwight Chapin "informed Haldeman that Graham wanted to be in touch with him and with the President. 'He is very disturbed,' Chapin reported, 'by some press reports which quote him as saying the war is deplorable.'"[203]

Later, as Watergate began to unravel the Nixon

presidency, Graham backpedaled from both the administration and his support for the war. "He told *The New York Times, Christianity Today,* and anyone else who asked, that in all the history of the Vietnam conflict, he had made only one public comment that could be construed as support for the war. ... Graham's critics were not impressed. Union Seminary's John C. Bennett observed that 'when people claim to be above politics it is axiomatic that they in effect support the status quo.'"[204]

Sometimes Graham's endorsement of law and order offered more than passive support of the status quo. In 1973, while visiting South Africa, Graham traded in Christian turn-the-other-cheek piety for Old Testament vengeance when he said, "I think when a person is found guilty of rape, he should be castrated. That would stop him pretty quick."[205] In the ensuing flap he backpedaled, explaining in his customary way that what he said did not "clarify my true thoughts."[206]

Such eye-for-an-eye justice harkened back to Graham's Bob Jones College days. He once recalled, "Cars of people from town came through the campus on Halloween night throwing firecrackers and rocks at the windows of our dorms. We knew they were going to be coming back, so the next night, a group of us boys hid behind some trees, and sure enough, here they came again, and as they were driving past us, we jumped out and let 'em have it with those rocks. I think we broke every window in those cars and cut those people all to pieces."[207]

In a similar vein, he reported years later about a basketball game date whom he abandoned to leap into a fist fight. "I was in the center of it all, and when one big fella came at me, I found a milk bottle and was able to break his head open. He left screaming, with blood running down his face. I thought maybe I had killed him, but on that night, as I recall it, I didn't mind if I had."[208]

On the other hand, his date recalled that he hadn't seemed mussed when he got back into the car and a former hand on his father's farm reported, "Billy, you know, was a leader, and leaders, you know, they never fight—they usually manage, if it has to come right down to that, to have somebody else sort of tend to that for them.„[209]

Nor was he reluctant to use a gun. While Graham was house-sitting for the Dean of Florida Bible Institute he kept a loaded 22 rifle at hand. Graham told a biographer that when someone banged on the door, "I figured this fella out there hollering he was Billy Graham had come to try to beat me up or something, was drunk or something, so I shot through the front door."[210] The presumptive assailant departed. This might be seen as a reflection of his broader view of retributive justice. Addressing the death penalty, he believed "when capital punishment is administered equally, it's proven to be a deterrent."[211]

In August of 1972, Graham advised Nixon that the bugging of the Watergate offices posed no problem with the electorate. He also reported in on his consultation with *Tonight Show* host Johnny Carson who was "trying to figure out how to help the President."[212]

Graham remained a Nixon supporter until tapes were released containing foul language, which apparently troubled the minister far more than the Watergate break-in or obstruction of justice. "I was terribly disappointed in those tapes. Just overwhelmingly sickened by them. Oh, the language." He went so far as to say, "The President never dreamed that he was being recorded."[213] This conveniently sidestepped the then-known fact that 24/7 recording in the Oval Office was a Nixon hallmark.

In 1998, Robert Sherrill noted in *The Nation*, "His deep loyalty to Nixon still surfaces when Graham laments, in almost every interview, that when the Watergate tapes were released, he was very offended by the cuss words. But that's all he mentions: just the profanity. He has never, not once, mentioned the taped evidence that Nixon was (expletive deleted) gung-ho for burglary, bribery, extortion and perjury."[214]

Notwithstanding Graham's hopeful view that Nixon's plummeting popularity in the wake of Watergate could be turned around, Nixon, facing impeachment, resigned on August 9, 1974. Gerald Ford took over the White House and the thankless task of extracting the U.S. from Vietnam. As U.S. troops were withdrawn from Southeast Asia in early 1975, North Vietnamese troops moved south. Hue, Da Nang and Ban Me Thuot fell in March, Xuan Loc in April, and Saigon on April 30. Ford declared the war "finished."

There has been much discussion of the so-called "Vietnam syndrome" in the ensuing three decades, usually cast in terms of either ignominious defeat of a superpower by guerillas or the sad failure of American leaders to acknowledge the will of another nation's people. There is a deeper issue however, which is rarely, if ever, addressed by most of Nixon's wartime supporters including Billy Graham. More than 20,000 U.S. soldiers died in Indochina between 1968 and 1975 together with at least a half-million Vietnamese, Laotian and Cambodian citizens obliterated with saturation bombing, chemical warfare and napalm. Agent Orange defoliant sprayed during those years and land mines laid are still taking their toll today. Yet the war was concluded on virtually the same terms Lyndon Johnson laid on the table in 1968, before Nixon secretly undermined negotiations. The blood of those hundreds of thousands, the sorrow chiseled into nearly half that somber black wall in Washington, is on Nixon's and Kissinger's hands. As Graham had truly observed in his rejoinder to Bishop Pike's pacifism, "There are millions of little people in Asia that are scared to death," but he mistook the enemy whom they most feared. Death rained down from B-52 bombers flying too high to be heard on the ground below while Graham opined that smoking and drinking were more urgent topics of ethical concern.

In neighboring Cambodia, the Khmer Rouge captured the capitol city of Phnom Penh on April 17 and on May 12 they seized the U.S. merchant ship *Mayaguez* in the Gulf of Siam about 60 miles from the Cambodian coastline.

That night at a crusade in Jackson, Miss., Graham asked, "What will the American response be? These things are happening all over the world, and the scriptures say there will come a day when the weak will say, 'I'm strong.' Those little nations will twist our tail and kick us and beat us, and there is nothing we can do about it; and we've already reached that stage." What translation of the scriptures contains this folksy prediction he did not say, but Graham was hot to throw some rocks. "I'm glad I'm not President—I tell you something would be done about it."[215]

Graham was presumably pleased with Ford's and Kissinger's response—two days later U.S. bombers were blasting mainland military targets at Kompong Som and Ream while Marines landed on the deck of the *Mayaguez* (to find it abandoned) and on Koh Tang Island where they met stiff resistance. Casualties were high—fifteen Marines died in the first hour of fighting and eight helicopters went down. Kissinger proposed dropping the largest bomb in the U.S. arsenal, a 15,000 pounder, on the tiny island. The White House announced that the invasion would end when the hostages were freed and the seamen were released an hour later. In the confusion of a hastily planned operation, directed as much at disproving superpower helplessness as at concrete results, three Marines were left behind on the island, presumably executed afterward. Of a total force of 110 Marines, 18 died, 50 were wounded and an additional 23 Air Force men died in a plane crash. Something had, indeed, been done.[216]

Like most right wing evangelicals, Graham's support for behavior-modifying laws included opposition to a woman's right to terminate an unwanted pregnancy. In 1975 Graham formed the Christian Action Council (which in 1995 changed its name to Care Net) with Dr. C. Everett Koop, and evangelists Harold O.J. Brown and Frances Schaeffer, to oppose abortion. The founders joined Catholics in their post-Roe v. Wade opposition efforts and the organization's Mission Statement states, "Care Net is a Christian ministry assisting and promoting the evangelistic, pro-life work of pregnancy centers in North America." Care Net's Web site claims to provide services for more than 1,000 Crisis Pregnancy Centers in the U.S. and Canada.

And again, like so many others on the political right, Graham's concern for life extended to the unborn but not the born. He always expressed allegiance to those in power and those who could advance his ministry whether their governments were democracies or dictatorships. As historian Gerald Colby noted, "Graham could even accept a former torturer from Uruguay's Death Squad, Nelson Bardesio, as an advance man for his Mexico

Crusade in 1977."[217]

Late in 1973, with Nixon disgraced and resigned and Gerald Ford in office, "Graham called to tell Ford that it would initiate a healing process if he pardoned Richard Nixon. Ford replied, 'Well, it's a tough call, a tough decision, there are many angles to it. I'm certainly giving it a lot of thought and prayer.' Graham said, 'Mr. President, I'm praying for you constantly.' Within a few days Ford announced a pardon for Nixon."[218]

Whether Ford's decision emanated from Graham's advice or that of the many Nixon loyalists who still populated the White House at the time, the pardon arguably torpedoed Ford's political career. Ford later said he had made up his mind before the Graham call. At the same time, the pardon may have emboldened others in his administration to regard the presidency as above the law—an attitude that would come back to bite the country when Dick Cheney and Donald Rumsfeld returned to power at the turn of the century.

"The shepherd always tries to persuade the sheep that their interests and his own are the same."

~Stendhal
(Marie-henri Beyle)

Chapter 16
Cross Purposes

Burned by his close association with Nixon, Graham retreated somewhat from public involvement with the presidency, a shift abetted by the election of two men who, for very different reasons, were less receptive to the reverend's desire for White House influence.

President Jimmy Carter's rise to national prominence was greatly aided by his being seen as the anti-Nixon. His perceived moral rectitude was an antidote to Watergate corruption. Graham's support would probably have contributed little to the electoral prospects of a plain spoken Sunday school teacher and Southern governor. At the same time, Carter embraced rather different religious views from the evangelist, despite the Bible-based faith they might appear to have held in common.

Graham was comfortable with the professed faith of men like Johnson or Nixon, who gave lip service to Christianity without apparently embracing much of Christ's teaching in the political arena. As became clear in retrospect, through tapes and diaries, neither man presented his true face to the public—true faces that must have been at least selectively familiar to an intimate like Graham. But Carter seemed to embody a very different ethos, wearing his faith on his sleeve.

According to Graham biographer Janet Lowe, "Graham once said of Carter: 'I would rather have a man in office who is highly qualified to be president who didn't make much of a religious profession than to have a man who had no qualifications but who made a religious profession.' Carter shot back: 'I think what people should look out for is people like Billy Graham, who go around telling people how to live their lives.'"[219] Other news stories attribute the rejoinder to Carter's son, Jeff, but the tone of the relationship was clearly unfriendly.

According to Vice President Walter Mondale, "Carter thought politics was sinful."[220] "After being denied a long list of federal appointments, an amazed House Democratic majority leader Jim Wright of Texas drawled, 'The president thought there was something tawdry—tawdry—about the idea of political appointments.'"[221] Graham, proponent of candidates and running mates, generals and judges, saw political appointments as part of his game.

Whereas Graham preached salvation through faith alone, Carter evinced belief in works, walking his talk to a degree unseen in other modern presidencies. Nixon had regularly cranked up the White House air conditioning while adding wood to the fireplace in summertime. Carter installed solar hot water panels, turned down the thermostat in winter and wore sweaters when he was chilly.

These practical differences manifested in political policy-making as well. Carter supported what fundamentalist Christians refer to as a secular humanist agenda—accepting the practical if lamentable benefit afforded by legal abortion, for example. On another front, while Graham claimed to oppose racial bias, his inner circle remained white and male but Carter appointed record numbers of women and minorities to significant government and judicial posts.

Due to such wide ranging differences, Graham rarely interacted with the White House during the Carter presidency. In 1979 Carter did seek Graham's help with Senate passage of the Strategic Arms Limitation Treaty he had negotiated with the Soviet Union. Graham had begun to argue for reduction of nuclear weapons after the National Council of Churches and the Southern Baptist Convention called for approval of SALT. Carter wanted Graham to testify before Congress and Graham declined. Though he had publicly voiced support for arms control, most notably on the CBS News with Walter Cronkite, Graham wasn't prepared to testify under oath. While some observers detected a change in his militaristic stance, a careful examination reveals that his position was more opportunistic than philosophical. The anti-nuclear mood was on the upswing around the world, but Graham remained adamant that he was not a pacifist.

Not long afterward he ramped up his fearmongering concerning the communist menace and told listeners that the country needed a strong leader to carry the coming battle. He had signed on with Ronald Reagan.

At that time Graham's evangelistic fundraising was paying huge dividends and drawing close scrutiny. Beginning in 1970, BGEA put millions into a spin-off, the World Evangelism and Christian Education Fund in Dallas. By the late 1970s WECEF had amassed $23 million in blue chips (including Exxon and IBM), bonds, land and cash.

In turn, BGEA and WECEF channeled millions to the Billy Graham Center at Wheaton College, *Christianity Today* Publications, *Christianity Today* International, The Cove Charitable Trust, World Wide Publishing, World Wide Pictures, Blue Ridge Broadcasting, Wycliffe Bible Translators, Campus Crusade and other evangelical groups. Massive expenditures for advertising were also channeled to Christian associates in Walter Bennett Communications, Fresh Air Media and DonorDirect.com.

Along the way, Graham's organization purchased land at an inflated price from Graham family associates for The Cove, also known as the Billy Graham Training Center, near Asheville. How much or whether Graham family members profited from the land deal is obscured by layers of contracts and corporate partnerships. An investigation by the *Charlotte Observer* raised significant questions about the propriety of the complicated scheme.

As reported by Robert Hodierne, WECEF paid $2.75 million for 1,050 acres of property. Just three months earlier, Pharr Yarns had paid $25,000 for a $2.1 million purchase option on the same land for which the highest previous offer had been $1.5 million. So Pharr's profit on the three month investment was $625,000. Was it simply luck?

Though neither Hodierne nor the IRS ever proved charges of collusion, serious questions were never resolved. William Pharr said he had shared the profit with McLain Hall, a Greenville, South Carolina, real estate broker. Hall and Melvin Graham, who speculated in land, were involved in several other deals at the time and Melvin sat on the WECEF board. Those other deals involved Pharr Yarns, Catherine Graham McElroy and Leighton Ford (an evangelist working under the BGEA umbrella) as well as Billy and Melvin's mother, Morrow. If Melvin conveyed information to Pharr, he violated the law. To make matters murkier, when all the numbers were crunched, $160,000 was missing.[222]

There have been no other substantive charges of financial wrongdoing on the part of Graham's organizations, and BGEA's books are regarded as transparent. However, it is far from clear that a full accounting has been made of all of Graham's financial affairs. Individual Limited Liability Corporations were created for many, perhaps most of his domestic crusades and campaigns. Such organizations are not legally sanctioned nonprofits, hence their books are not open for inspection. The LLCs are disbanded after each event. Graham's ownership of a luxurious vacation home in the country club community of Pauma Valley, California doesn't show up on the San Diego County tax records under his or any of his nonprofit organization's names. Though Hodierne focussed on The Cove property, BGEA and its offshoots own hundreds of millions of dollars worth of property directly and there is no way to estimate the holdings of associates and arms-length businesses.

While it is true that many in Graham's constituency had voted for Carter in 1976, that support quickly faded. Carter claimed ten of the eleven southern states in his 1976 victory over Gerald Ford, but failed to win any state other than his native Georgia in his 1980 loss to Ronald Reagan. Part and parcel of that shift was the rise of a movement which called itself the New Right and the formation of a raft of new religion-based political action groups in the late 1970s.

As noted by historian Kevin Phillips, "The National Federation for Decency (1977), evangelist Jerry Falwell's Moral Majority (1979), the Religious Roundtable (1979), the *Christian Voice* (1979), the National Affairs Briefing (1980), the Council on Revival (1980), and the Council for National Policy (1981)," took the stage.[223] These heirs to Graham's back room machinations felt no need to mask their political involvement. Jerry Falwell, Paul Weyrich (an Eastern Orthodox Republican political organizer) and William W. Pennell (a Baptist minister) led the charge against Carter, with televangelist Pat Robertson in their wake.

In 1980 the Southern Baptist Convention turned on Carter, calling his White House Conference on the Family, "a general undermining of the biblical concept of family."[224] Meanwhile, Reagan was courting the SBC and all of the new politically active religious groups with general affirmations of support.

As reported by Rowland Evans and Robert Novak, the Moral Majority's views could have been lifted directly from Graham's sermons since 1949. "To the fundamentalists, the great Satan abroad was godless Communism, centered in Moscow. At home, Satan was the antifamily counterculture of drugs, pornography and godlessness." As Evans and Novak observed, "Carter failed the test of the preachers on these social questions as badly as on his foreign policy. They felt the President had sold them out on abortion, the Equal Rights Amendment, private schools, homosexuals and school prayer."[225]

The 1980s saw the rise of Christian television networks as a potent social force. Robertson had created the Christian Broadcasting Network in 1961 with his flagship show, *The 700 Club,* where Jim and Tammy Faye Bakker launched their careers, later joining the Trinity Broadcasting Network to pilot their ill-fated PTL (Praise the Lord) ministry. PTL ran afoul of the IRS and was charged with bilking investors. Falwell's Moral Majority assumed control of PTL after the Bakkers' fall from grace, but it soon collapsed in bankruptcy. Sporadic TV extravaganzas showcasing Graham's crusades and regular broadcast of Sunday sermons had finally emerged as daily programming at stations across the country.

Another potent media effort, *Focus on the Family,* was initiated in 1977 and its radio audience swelled through the Reagan years. Founder James Dobson was unabashed in using his electronic pulpit to lobby for social conservatism and political action.

Ronald Reagan was diffident about religion, proudly pro-union and decidedly humanist during his career in Hollywood and early years in California politics, but he moved right and warmed to religionists' power if not their beliefs immediately before and during his eight years in the governor's mansion. And he was at least well acquainted with Graham. One biographer notes, "Billy met Ronald Reagan a year after he married Nancy. [1952]... Reagan and Billy have been close friends ever since."[226]

When he became California's governor in 1967, Reagan announced that he wanted to run the office according to the teachings of Jesus and twice invited Graham to address the state legislature. "[Reagan] asked him to discuss with his California cabinet the second coming of Christ."[227] In 1969 Reagan attended Graham's Anaheim crusade and lent his imprimatur to the enterprise, noting, "I'm sure there will be those who question my participation here tonight. People have become so concerned with church-state separation that we have interpreted freedom of religion into freedom from religion."[228]

By the time Reagan began his run for the White House he was comfortably expressing views confluent with the Moral Majority. In 1980 he told a meeting of evangelicals, "I know you can't endorse me, but I want you to know that I endorse you and what you are doing."[229] Soon their disquiet with Carter policies moved them into solid support for the Republican rival and they helped put Reagan into the White House.

Reagan's electoral success was substantially abetted by Iranian supporters of Ayatollah Khomeini who had captured a large group of American diplomatic corps members and held them hostage for months. Carter first ordered a military rescue which failed when helicopters went down in the Iranian desert and then attempted a diplomatic solution. When a settlement appeared close at hand before the 1980 presidential election, Reagan's allies, including George H.W. Bush, Bill Casey and others with CIA connections, are alleged to have secretly offered the Iranians aid and arms in exchange for extending the captivity past election day. Although specific allegations were investigated and dismissed by House and Senate committees as well as a handful of news organizations, the fact that there were high level contacts between Republican operatives and Iranian officials remains undisputed.

Reporter Gary Sick who investigated and reported those contacts in *October Surprise: America's Hostages in Iran and the Election of Ronald Reagan* (Random House/Times Books,

1991), later acknowledged that the congressional inquiry had failed to establish a quid pro quo but insisted that further investigation was warranted. Writers Kevin Phillips, David Corn, Robert Parry and others continue to endorse the allegations and new information continues to surface. At least one of the first-hand witnesses called in the special prosecutors' investigation failed a lie detector test when he denied the existence of such a deal.[230] Six years later an illegal arms-for-hostages deal with Iran, as well as illegal funding of the Contra revolutionaries in Nicaragua, became known as the Iran-Contra affair. The lead players in Iran were the same figures previously associated with the alleged election-eve bargain and Reagan administration members established beyond doubt that they were willing to violate the law to advance political goals.

First Lady Nancy Reagan famously (or infamously) sought spiritual and practical advice from astrologers and planned her husband's itinerary based on the stars, which had a dampening effect on evangelical support. But as long as policy decisions trended in their direction, the religious faction was generally willing to chalk it up to the First Lady's nuttiness.

During the Reagan presidency Graham regained some of his access and influence in the White House and later stated that, of all the presidents he was closest to Reagan. He played his accustomed role as presidential apple-polisher when he told Reagan, "I would think that you have talked about God more than any other president since Abraham Lincoln."[231]

Graham broke with Reagan when he decided to take his crusade to the Soviet Union, a move the President opposed. But the lure of a new and certainly profitable market behind the Iron Curtain proved more attractive than approval from the White House.

While Graham would later tell interviewers that he was closer to Reagan than to any other president, that sense of intimacy is missing from Reagan's memoirs. In almost eight hundred pages of Reagan's recently published diaries, Graham is only mentioned in passing: a character attending various state functions or source of glowing praise for presidential godliness.

Nor are there any photographs of Graham among hundreds offered up on the Reagan Library Web site. In the book, the only comment on other subjects credited to the evangelist is that he "questioned the status of Desmond Tutu." There is no explanatory material concerning Graham's reasons for doubting the stature of a man who had then been awarded a Nobel Peace Prize and the Albert Schweitzer prize for Humanitarianism.

"War is a racket. It is the only one international in scope. It is the only one in which the profits are reckoned in dollars and the losses in lives."

~General Smedley Butler

Chapter 17
The Saudi Connection

Ronald Reagan was a fearmonger par excellence and his style would become a blueprint for the younger Bush when he seized the presidency twenty years later. While working to crush organized labor, roll back social welfare programs and cut taxes on the rich, Reagan worked the American public like a stage magician, keeping audience attention on a string of trumped up threats around the globe. The invasion of Grenada, an essentially unarmed country that supposedly posed a military threat to the U.S., was coupled with constant warnings that Nicaragua's socialist government wanted to invade Texas. Castro continued to be vilified while American bombers unloaded over Grenada (1983), Lebanon (1983, 1984—both Lebanese and Syrian targets), Libya (1986), El Salvador and Nicaragua (throughout the 1980s) and Iran (1987). In addition, the Reagan administration continued and escalated Carter's interventions in Angola, East Timor, Seychelles, South Yemen and Afghanistan while adding El Salvador, Honduras, Chad and Suriname. As always, support for Israel was unwavering. Perhaps constant warring spurred the frequent references to God that Graham found so laudable.

Though other evangelical voices clamoring for Reagan's ear were united in their unqualified support for Israel, Graham worked at cross purposes with his competitors in at least one instance. "Columnists Rowland Evans and Robert Novak reported that in the fall of 1981 Graham successfully lobbied several key senators on behalf of the President's plan to sell AWACS [Airborne Warning and Control Systems] airplanes to Saudi Arabia, a measure actively opposed by Jerry Falwell and his avidly pro-Israel troops in the Moral Majority. Graham minimized his role, but did not deny that at the President's request he had indicated to several legislators that putting AWACS in Saudi hands posed no military threat to Israel."[232]

Graham's less public posture resulted in a less visible historical trail. Did Reagan just happen to call on the evangelist to further a single arms deal? Was it a one-time task undertaken to establish his worth as a political operative? Is this the only such effort that came to light, lifting it from a background of close collaboration behind the scenes? Or was Graham working on behalf of his allies at Boeing, Grumman and Westinghouse?

Graham had earlier established a friendship with CIA Director George Herbert Walker Bush, now become Reagan's Vice President. Bush, with close ties to Saudi Arabia's petroleum princes, could easily have masterminded the AWACS deal.

During the Reagan presidency, Graham's son Franklin was deeply enmeshed with the Contras, a military group waging war against the popularly elected Sandanista government of Nicaragua. The revolutionary army was funded illegally by administration operatives through arms sales to Iran in what became known as the Iran-Contra Scandal. Congress had explicitly banned arms trade with Iran and all aid to the revolutionaries in Nicaragua. Reagan's and Bush's illegal operation ended with multiple indictments and convictions of many of the principal players in Washington. Reagan said Bush was party to all of the dealing but his vice president maintained "plausible deniability" and Reagan explained everything away as a simple oversight on his part. Franklin visited Contra encampments in Honduras, trained chaplains for the civil war effort and vilified the Sandanistas as godless communists.[233]

In a media coup reminiscent of Hearst's 1949 "puff Graham" telegram to his editors, the world's most powerful right-wing publisher, Rupert Murdoch, joined the Graham publicity team in 1984 in the lead-up to a series of European crusades. As reported in *Christianity Today*, "Before the crusades began, controversial newspaper publisher Rupert Murdoch, owner of tabloids in England and the United States, called a meeting to introduce his London editors to Graham. The following month, one of Murdoch's papers and England's largest, *The Sun*, editorialized that Graham 'would make a wonderful bishop' and an even better archbishop in the Church of England."[234]

In April of the following year, signaling the importance he attached to Christian political activism, Graham told Pat Robertson's *700 Club* television audience that: "The time has come when evangelicals are going to have to think about getting organized corporately... I'm for evangelicals running for public office and winning if possible and getting control of the Congress, getting control of the bureaucracy, getting control of the executive branch of government. I think if we leave it to the other side we're going to be lost. I would like to see every true believer involved in politics in some way shape or form."[235] Two decades later, evangelical political activism would be credited by many with positioning George W. Bush for appointment to the presidency by a compliant Supreme Court followed by his appropriation of a second term.

It was in 1985 that Graham's message of salvation reached his most famous convert. As reported in *The New York Times*, "Instead of learning the limitations of his Harvard training, what George W. Bush learned instead during these fitful years were lessons about faith and its particular efficacy. It was in 1985, around the time of his 39th birthday, George W. Bush says, that his life took a sharp turn toward salvation ... Several accounts have emerged from those close to Bush about a faith 'intervention' of sorts at the Kennebunkport family compound that year. Details vary, but here's the gist of what I understand took place. George W., drunk at a party, crudely insulted a friend of his mother's. George senior and Barbara blew up. Words were exchanged along the lines of something having to be done. George senior, then the vice president, dialed up his friend, Billy Graham, who came to the compound and spent several days with George W. in probing exchanges and walks on the beach. George W. was soon born again. He stopped drinking, attended Bible study and wrestled with issues of fervent faith. A man who was lost was saved."[236]

Some might find it amusing that recurrent DWIs and cocaine use not to mention his absence without leave from the Air National Guard during 16 months of the Vietnam war (as accurately reported by Dan Rather and CBS News*), didn't call for parental control, but a drunken insult demanded a seaside revival. The rich, as they say, are different.

A PBS Frontline program, "The Jesus Factor," presented its version of Bush's conversion. He was raised an Episcopalian and became a Methodist when he married; by the mid-'80s he was drinking, his marriage was on the rocks, his career was listless. As Bush explained with his customary agrammatical aplomb, "One day I spent a weekend with the great Billy Graham."

Graham, for his part, has publicly downplayed his role in G.W.'s conversion, but his suasion and that of his son and G.W.'s peer, Franklin, would be apparent when the younger Bush took his turn in Washington.

Whatever the preacher's influence or function might have been behind the scenes, the public record of personal contact through the Reagan presidency is thin. There were occasional White House visits and the minister is said to have rushed to Washington to comfort the First Lady following the attempted presidential assassination. But, according to Christianity Today, "Indeed, in 1989, Graham said he no longer frequented the halls of Congress and the White House because he believed God had 'called him to a much higher calling.'"[237] Another interpretation would be that the White House had stopped calling him, but that would soon change with the ascendancy of G.H.W. Bush.

*Rather was drummed out of his job due to a reportorial technicality, despite the fact that his story turned out to be accurate. The provvenance of the documents on which Rather's story relied was called into question, but all subsequent investigation showed that Bush skipped out on his service obligations. Bush's official records from that period were, reportedly, accidentally destroyed.

Cecil Bothwell 147

"The urge to save humanity is almost always only a false-face for the urge to rule it."

~**H. L. Mencken**

Chapter 18
Saddam is the Antichrist

"In 1991, Graham told an interviewer that he regretted 'the politics part' of his relationship with Nixon, and Graham insiders report that ever since the deep disappointments of Watergate, the evangelist has made a point of limiting his discussion and counsel to spiritual topics and prayer."[238] However, the United Nations deadline for Saddam's withdrawal from Kuwait was nine days away when George H.W. Bush taped this audio diary entry on January 6, 1991.

"A very supportive phone call from Billy Graham. He quotes from James Russell Lowell's poem, 'The Present Crisis.' 'Once to every man and nation comes the moment to decide and the choice goes by forever, twixt that darkness and that light.' It does hit me pretty hard -- that moment's upon us.

"Prayer is important. ... Billy Graham offers his help and talks about Saddam Hussein being the Antichrist itself. This is the most momentous decision facing a President in modern times. [Billy] wants to speak out in any way he can, and that would indeed be helpful." (Ellipsis and brackets are verbatim from Bush's written transcript of his audio diary.)[239]

Reading past Bush's self-aggrandizement we here see Graham egging the president on in much the same way he had encouraged Johnson's war effort in 1965. It isn't possible to infer from the context of Bush's abridged recitation of the poem whether it represents his own or Graham's edit. The line is actually an excerpt from "Once To Every Man and Nation" not "The Present Crisis," (written three years earlier). This mistake of title, whether by Bush or Graham, was doubtless suggested by the imminence of war with Iraq following its invasion of Kuwait.

Ironically, Lowell was an ardent abolitionist and his florid verse was written in protest of the U.S. war on Mexico and published in the *Boston Courier* in 1848. Taken as a whole, the poem condemns the justification of war through falsehood while urging the embrace of truth even if it is costly to reputation or wallet. Lowell was convinced, with considerable reason, that the intent of the Mexican war was to expand slave territory. It is difficult, sans abridgment, to read it as an incitement to war.

Use of the Antichrist label is not unique to Graham, of course, nor even to Graham vis-à-vis Saddam. He had branded communism with the epithet in the 1950s. Other proponents of Christian empire through the ages have pasted opposition leaders with the title: English, Dutch and Lutheran religious leaders so labeled King Phillip II of Spain after defeat of the armada in 1588; and Dutch Reformed ministers called Louis XIV, of France, the Antichrist a century later; while not a few have used the appellation to describe Adolf Hitler or Joseph Stalin or Mao Zedong.

Though Tim Lahaye's and Jerry Jenkins' first *Left Behind* novel wouldn't be published for another four years, Graham's message could have been lifted directly from that series, which posits a Mideast dictator as the antichrist. As Kevin Phillips notes, "Still others pondered whether the antichrist was already alive and who he might be. (Saddam Hussein himself was a frequent choice.)"[240]

As to Graham's counsel for war, if such advice constitutes "spiritual topics and prayer," that topic is widely drawn indeed. Soon Bush told his staff, "I've resolved all the moral issues in my mind. It's black and white, good versus evil."[241] "In a speech January 16, 1991, Billy Graham declared: 'There come times when we have to fight for peace.' He went on to say that out of the present war in the Gulf may 'come a new peace and, as suggested by the President, a new world order.'"[242]

Graham's version of events during that week differed somewhat from the President's diary entry. Graham told *People* magazine that "George Bush asked him to come to Washington, D.C. [on Jan. 16], *but did not say why*." (italics added)

"'They put me in the Lincoln Room,' Graham recalls, 'and all of a sudden there came a knock at the door. There was Mrs. Bush ...'"[243] She invited him up to the Blue Room to watch TV.

People reported: "They turned on CNN and watched the beginning of the air war against Iraq,"[244] and that Graham said the three prayed together three times that evening before Bush delivered a televised message to the nation.

Other versions of the story suggest that Graham finessed his report of the Presidential presence in the Blue Room. Historian William Doyle reported that "George Bush sat in the small private study next to the Oval Office with his top White House aides, firing a remote control at the TV"[245] as the first bombs fell on Baghdad. The scene was recorded on videotape.

A contemporaneous report in *Christianity Today* noted that Graham "emphasized the complexity of the situation. 'No sane person wants war. At the same time, it has well been said that there is an ethical responsibility that goes with power, and sometimes it becomes necessary to fight the strong in order to protect the weak,' he said. Whatever the final outcome of the hostilities, Graham said, God has ultimate control. Graham said the world will never be the same after this confrontation in the Middle East because of its strategic location. Not only does the crisis affect every person economically, politically, and socially, but the situation has major spiritual implications as well, he said. 'These events are happening in that part of the world where history began, and, the Bible says, where history as we know it will some day end," Graham said. "I believe there are some spiritual forces at work -- both good and evil -- that are beyond our comprehension.' In addition to offering comfort and counsel to Bush, Graham participated in Washington-area religious services focused on the conflict."[246]

Two months earlier, *U.S. News & World Report* had noted, "The Rev. Billy Graham, preaching to a crowd of about 20,000 in Long Island, N.Y., warned there are 'spiritual forces at work' in the Persian Gulf confrontation. 'History has gone full circle, and we are coming back to these [Bible] lands,' said Graham. 'This is not another Korea, it is not another Vietnam -- it is something far more sinister and far more difficult.'"[247]

At the end of the decade, *Time* magazine reported in "The Time 100: The most important people of the century," "Graham's finest moment may have been when he appeared at President Bush's side, Bible in hand, as we commenced our war against Iraq in 1991. The great revivalist's presence symbolized that the Gulf crusade was, if not Christian, at least biblical."[248] Taken another way, the revivalist's presence was, if not narrowly partisan, at least geopolitical.

For Graham and other believers in Armageddon, the prospect of war in the Mideast offered a better fit with apocalyptic preachments drawn from Judeo-Christian texts than conflicts elsewhere, though connection to that region was never an absolute requirement. Israel's creation by the United Nations had offered a sure sign of the end times but Stalin and world communism were labeled "the Antichrist" and the Book of Revelations was reinterpreted to include the Soviet Union, at least until Mikhail Gorbachev inconveniently permitted its dissolution. Graham said the future of Christianity was on the line in Korea and that Eisenhower or Truman might be the "last president" but later there was, ominously, "more at stake" in Vietnam than anyone realized. America's reinstallation of the Shah in Iran was obviously a Biblical sign, or maybe it was his exile that proved the rule. Eisenhower, Kennedy, Johnson, Nixon and G.H.W. Bush had each been tapped by Graham (for God) to be the saviors of the world or the Western world or, perhaps, Christendom. Like millennial cults through the ages, when one prophesied deadline or Great Satan came and went, the prophecy was simply recast as another proof of faith or lack of faith or fallacy or inerrancy, probable proof of Jesus' love, evidence of divine disfavor or favor. The faithful were ever willing to follow.

Cecil Bothwell 153

"So convenient a thing it is to be a *reasonable Creature*, since it enables one to find or make a Reason for everything one has a mind to do."

~**Benjamin Franklin**

Chapter 19
Endorsing persecution

Following the 1992 election of Bill Clinton, a crisis erupted over North Korean plutonium production. The Clinton administration was determined to prevent Kim Il Sung from acquiring nuclear weapons. As the crisis escalated with no apparent flexibility on Kim's part, the President dispatched Billy Graham to Pyongyang with a "resolute note from Clinton in hand. The essence of the American message: cooperate on the nuclear issue immediately or face dire consequences."[249]

Echoing the note on which he had launched his White House campaign forty-three years earlier with the Truman telegram urging a Korean invasion, Graham had now become the Presidential messenger conveying a threat of war. Graham returned home empty-handed and the two nations engaged in a chess game of brinksmanship. Clinton had painted Kim into a corner and left him no honorable way out. Finally, Jimmy Carter convinced Vice President Al Gore to talk Clinton into letting him travel to North Korea and Carter was able to defuse the pending explosion.

When Clinton's Asia policies were questioned in 1998, he joined his Presidential predecessors in welcoming Graham's imprimatur. In advance of his trip to China that summer, Clinton said, "This policy is supported by our key democratic allies in Asia, Japan, South Korea, Australia, Thailand, the Philippines. It has recently been publicly endorsed by a number of distinguished religious leaders, including Reverend Billy Graham and the Dalai Lama."[250]

When Clinton was under attack for his dalliance with a White House intern, Monica Lewinsky, Graham stood up for him in what might be interpreted as a defense of sin. He told the press, "[Clinton] 'is a strong and vigorous young man' with 'such a tremendous personality' that 'the ladies just go wild over him' and 'he's had a lot of temptations thrown his way and a lot of pressure on him. Oh, it must be tough. I know how hard it is.'"[251] Presumably, Graham meant that women go wild over him, too.

Hillary Clinton said that Graham was of considerable help to her in weathering the public and private storms attendant to the Lewinsky affair and impeachment proceedings. Perhaps surprisingly, Hillary's theological consanguinity with Graham may be more substantial than his relationship with most or all of the presidents. Her religious attachments in Washington have been decidedly conservative and fundamentalist.

During Bill Clinton's White House years, Hillary was a regular member of the Fellowship, a network of sex-segregated cells of political, business and military leaders. Writing in *Mother Jones* (September-October, 2007), Kathryn Joyce and Jeff Sharlet reported that her cell included: Susan Baker, wife of G.H.W. Bush consigliere James Baker; Joanne Kemp, wife of conservative icon Jack Kemp; Eileen Bakke, wife of Dennis Bakke, a leader in the anti-union Christian management movement; and Grace Nelson, the wife of Senator Bill Nelson, a conservative Florida Democrat. Other Washington figures involved in the Fellowship include John Ashcroft, Senator George Allen, Edwin Meese III, Senator Joe Lieberman, Senator Sam Brownback, Senator James Inhofe and Senator Tom Coburn. The politics and religion are decidedly right-wing. As Joyce and Sharlet reported, the semi-secret organization is dedicated to "spiritual war" on behalf of Christ and believes that the elite win power by the will of God. Such tenets couldn't be more compatible with those of Graham and his assertion that governments are always instruments of God. (Sharlet later published more complete coverage in *The Family: The Secret Fundamentalism at the Heart of American Power*: Harper-Collins, 2008, and *C Street: The Fundamentalist Threat to American Democracy*; Little Brown, *2010*.)

The years may have slowed Graham down, but his sermons were still laced with the hawkish rhetoric of the 1950s, as when he told a group of Promise Keepers in 1997, "God is not calling us to a playground. He is calling us to a battleground. This is warfare and we are in the center of the battle."[252] In *Approaching Hoofbeats: The Four Horsemen of the Apocalypse*

(1983), an end-is-near book of warnings and ramblings clearly intended to frighten readers into the penstock of promised salvation, Graham wrote: "… we should urge all governments to respect the rights of religious believers as outlined in the United Nations Declaration of Human Rights. We must hope that some day all nations (as all those who signed the Final Act of Helsinki declared) 'will recognize and respect the freedom of the individual to profess and practice, alone or in community with others, religion or belief acting in accordance with the dictates of his own conscience' (Final Act of Helsinki, section VII)."[253]

While the rights of religious believers might appear to be an obvious bottom line for an evangelist intent on increasing his flock, fifteen years later Graham had evidently changed his mind —at least when the choice was between religious freedom and business profits. Graham linked arms with multinational corporations to oppose economic sanctions designed to enforce the U.N. declaration.

In the late twentieth century the world community began to use sanctions to shape policy in nations which committed egregious human rights violations. Economic sanctions helped end apartheid in South Africa, for example, and may have moved Muamar Ghaddafi to cooperate with investigation of the Pan Am 103 downing in Lockerbie, Scotland. Sanctions prevented Saddam Hussein from rearming after the first Gulf War as well. By the 1990s, human rights activists in concert with a Democratic majority in Congress, were pressing for U.S. sanctions against the worst offenders including Burma, Haiti, Nigeria and Uzbekistan.

Many corporations, valuing profit above human rights, vehemently oppose sanctions, particularly unilateral rules which they claim hurt U.S. business interests and give unsanctioned foreign competitors an advantage. This viewpoint has enjoyed vocal political support in high places (none more vociferous than Vice President Dick Cheney).

In 1995, Clinton signed an Executive Order prohibiting U.S. companies from doing business with Iran, a prohibition strengthened by Congress the following year with passage of the Iran Libya Sanctions Act. Former Secretary of Defense Cheney was then CEO of Halliburton, which already faced fines for violation of the U.S. Export Administration Act for illegal sales to

Iran in 1993 and 1994. Unabashed, Cheney sought a waiver from ILSA regulations and, when rejected, used shell companies to engage in proscribed trade with Iraq and Iran. Halliburton subsidiaries traded with some of the worst of the worst, including Azerbaijan, Burma, Indonesia, Libya and Nigeria, while Cheney defended the practice. "We go where the business is,"[254] he said. To further oppose sanctions, Halliburton cofounded USA ENGAGE with Unocal in 1997, a group joined by over 600 other big businesses including Boeing, Caterpillar, Northrup Grumman, Westinghouse, IBM, and Mobil. The group rapidly became the leading lobbying group against sanctions.

The well-funded campaign soon began to target specific policies, using the wedge issue playbook developed by Newt Gingrich and other right-wing politicians as part of their Contract With America campaign in 1994. By 1998, according to a report by Jacob Heilbrunn writing for *The New Republic,* "the main preoccupation of sanction opponents is the Religious Persecution Act." USA ENGAGE's allies in opposing the Act included Billy Graham and the National Council of Churches. The surprising argument offered by these religious leaders was "that acts which might be seen as 'persecution' could really be an attempt to 'preserve authentic religious and cultural traditions.'"[255] The coalition was successful in killing the legislation.

Clearly, Graham's opposition to the law was for the benefit of the Billy Graham Evangelical Association and its associated companies whose vast financial holdings included investments in arms manufacture and oil. Multinational corporations including Exxon and IBM, represented in portfolios of the BGEA and its related investment arms are the very businesses most affected by sanctions, depending as they do on free and wholly unfettered international trade, particularly trade in weapons.

"I increasingly regard the church as an institution which defended such evils as slavery, color, caste, exploitation of labor and war."

~W.E.B. Dubois

Chapter 20
A new crusade

Two days before the 2000 election, Graham appeared with George W. Bush in Florida, and offered what was widely understood to be an endorsement. He spoke of his long friendship with the Bush family and said, "I had the privilege of leading the inaugural prayer when he was inaugurated Governor of Texas. And I have been praying for this crucial election. And I think it's a crucial election, a critical election in the history of America. And I think that, uh, I've been praying that God's will shall be done." Offering a disingenuous disclaimer he went on, "I don't endorse candidates. But I've come as close to it, I guess, now as any time in my life, because I think it's extremely important. We have in our state absentee voting. I've already voted. I'll just let you guess who I voted for. And my family the same way. And we believe that there's going to be a tremendous victory and change by Tuesday night in the direction of the country. Putting it in good hands. I believe in the integrity of this man. I've known him as a boy, I've known him as a young man, I've known him now still as a young man. And we're very proud of him. I'm very thankful for the privilege of calling him friend, and his wife. It's worth getting him the White House to get her in the White House ... Laura is a special person, I can tell you ... And if they, by God's will, win, I'm going to do everything in my power to help them make it a successful presidency. God bless all of you."[256]

Florida was a must-win state for Bush, and though post-election tabulations by a newspaper consortium would eventually establish that he lost the state, Graham's endorsement surely helped the Republican Party in its successful electoral and post-electoral machinations and successful Supreme Court battle for victory.

With the Bush ascension, Graham's White House influence would seem to have reached its apogee; a man he had personally led to Christ would now lead the nation. As an elder, Graham doesn't appear to enjoy as close a personal relationship to the younger Bush as to his father, but Graham's son Franklin is a G.W. Bush confidant and delivered the sermon at the 2001 inauguration.

In some measure, Franklin's involvement probably partakes of tradition, both in name and function, since he now heads up the BGEA. Moreover, Franklin and G.W. are close in age and share the experience of reprobate youth: hard drinking (and drugs?), fast cars, women, and abrupt embrace of Christianity in adulthood. Both skipped active military service, as well, though Bush enlisted in the Air National Guard and reputedly showed up from time to time. According to the White House, Bush's military records were accidentally destroyed, so his attendance or lack thereof cannot be documented, despite statements by officers and acquaintances who affirm his absence without leave.

However, following the events of 9/11, Bush bypassed camaraderie in favor of star-power when he needed blessing for an incipient crusade. The elder Graham was one of the clergymen who spoke in the National Cathedral on Sept. 14, 2001, an occasion when Bush delivered a war speech in church, saying "This conflict was begun on the timing and terms of others. It will end in a way, and at an hour, of our choosing."[257]

Graham, as ever, offered God's imprimatur to the new American war, saying, "We've always needed God from the very beginning of this nation, but today we need Him especially. We're facing a new kind of enemy. We're involved in a new kind of warfare. And we need the help of the Spirit of God." He concluded by conferring his blessing on Bush. "We also know that God is going to give wisdom, and courage, and strength to the President, and those around him. And this is going to be a day that we will remember as a day of victory. May God bless you all."[258]

As reported by Ron Suskind in *The New York Times,* "It was during a press conference on Sept. 16, in response to a question about homeland security efforts infringing on civil rights, that Bush first used the telltale word "crusade" in public.

'This is a new kind of - a new kind of evil,' he said. 'And we understand. And the American people are beginning to understand. This crusade, this war on terrorism is going to take a while.'"[259]

Theologian and columnist James Carroll wrote, in the *Boston Globe,* of Graham's involvement: "The old time political religion woke up, and Billy Graham was still there to preach it. Graham did not expressly name the new enemy, but his son and successor Franklin did, labeling Islam a 'very evil and wicked religion.' The unleashed energy of an exclusivist doctrine of salvation led, as always, to the denigration of those who are not among the saved, and, in the context of political emergency, that denigration has again become violent. Bush's war is a religious war, whether he disavows 'crusade' or not ... Billy Graham is a lion-hearted American, and one can only wish him well. But the implications of his transcending influence, old and new, should not be ignored. More than the man himself, the nation's response to him and his themes tells us who we are."[260]

Carroll continued, "Graham had his finger on the pulse of American fear, and in subsequent years, anti-communism occupied the nation's soul as an avowedly religious obsession. The Red scare at home, unabashed moves toward empire abroad, the phrase 'under God' inserted into the Pledge of Allegiance, the scapegoating of homosexuals as 'security risks,' an insane accumulation of nuclear weapons, suicidal wars against postcolonial insurgencies in Asia—a set of desperate choices indeed. Through it all, Billy Graham was the high priest of the American crusade, which is why U.S. presidents uniformly sought his blessing."[261]

As Americans belatedly acquired a smattering of awareness about Islam, Bush located Afghanistan and Iraq on a map and launched his global crusade. According to a *Newsweek* report published in 2006, Graham considered phoning the geopolitically challenged President "to advise him on the difference between Sunnis and Shiites, but decided against it." Meanwhile, Graham's mouthpiece, *Christianity Today,* began a litany of endorsements for the war. "The struggle must be waged on a variety of fronts: Christians praying always and everywhere;

missionaries and local believers hazarding their lives in sharing the gospel in the most religiously repressive settings; relief agencies and local congregations refusing to discriminate in distributing aid to the needy; Christian diplomats employing all the wiles of their craft; and, yes, Christian fighter pilots, navy personnel, and infantry insisting, when other options are exhausted and military force is called for, that liberty must be respected and justice done ... with sadness, realizing that on this side of the kingdom, justice is often impossible without some violence ..."262

Post-9/11 politics became, for politicians seeking to capitalize on the disaster, an explicit exercise in fear. The Department of Homeland Security was created and rapidly developed into the largest agency of the government, its very name calling up phantoms of mid-century Germany and reinforcing feelings of insecurity in the populace. Former National Security Adviser Zbigniew Brzezinski observed, "The war on terror feeds on fear and ambiguity." He argued that declaration of war on terror is vacuous and misdirects both the government and the people. "Terror is a technique for killing people. It doesn't tell you who you're fighting or who your allies are ... I see signs on the highway that read, 'Report suspicious activity.' It sounds like Orwell. This propagation of fear at the highest level, I find destructive."263

Two weeks later, *Christianity Today* editorialized, "We recognize the moral justness of the war on terrorism and have lent our support to it."264 And again the following June, "[T]he U.S. would be unforgivably selfish if it did not continue to risk using its God-given power and influence to try to 'bring liberty to the captives' in other lands."265 The magazine had also reminded its readers that Mohammed had instructed his followers: "The sword is the key of heaven and hell; a drop of blood shed in the cause of Allah, a night spent in arms, is of more avail than two months of fasting or prayer: whosoever falls in battle, his sins are forgiven, and at the day of judgment his limbs shall be supplied by the wings of angels and cherubims."266

The passage recalls the 1966 Washington prayer breakfast when Graham preached, "Jesus said, 'Think not that I am come to send peace on earth: I came not to send peace but a sword.' There are those who have tried to reduce Christ to the level of a genial and innocuous appeaser; but Jesus said 'You are wrong -- I have come as a fire-setter and a sword-wielder.'"

It was seven years later that French ex-President Jacques Chirac confirmed the extent of religious influence in the Bush administration's war plans. French journalist Jean-Claude Maurice, related an interview with Chirac in his book, *Si Vous le Répétez, Je Démentirai (If You Repeat it, I Will Deny);* (Plon, 2009).

Chirac told Maurice that the American leader appealed to their "common faith" (Christianity) and told him: "Gog and Magog are at work in the Middle East.... The biblical prophecies are being fulfilled.... This confrontation is willed by God, who wants to use this conflict to erase his people's enemies before a New Age begins."

The French leader said the conversation occurred in 2003 while the White House was assembling its "coalition of the willing" to unleash the Iraq invasion. Chirac noted that he was astonished by Bush's call and "wondered how someone could be so superficial and fanatical in their beliefs."

"I almost shudder at the thought of alluding to the most fatal example of the abuses of grief which the history of mankind has preserved—the Cross. Consider what calamities that engine of grief has produced!"

~John Adams
Letter to Thomas Jefferson

Chapter 21
The Prince of War

Today Graham's numerous imitators enjoy considerable influence, particularly within the Republican party though there are also many Democrats who feel called to offer lip service, at least, to Christian dogma. Many among them claim that a "family values" campaign provided Bush's margin of victory in the 2004 presidential election. Most have been vocal supporters of the administration's wars in Afghanistan and Iraq. Graham's direct heir, Franklin, is even more hawkish than his father and has admitted, "War satisfies my need for danger."[267]

Franklin's Samaritan's Purse organizations deliver translated Bibles, medicine and food to crisis zones and that work has taken him to Bosnia, Haiti, Ethiopia and other hot spots. In his autobiography, *Rebel with a Cause,* he claimed he dodged Israeli and Palestinian Liberation Organization cannon fire in Beirut and made risky forays into Honduras during the Nicaraguan civil war.

The exception to the younger Graham's taste for battle came during the elder Bush's Gulf War. Franklin initially endorsed Saddam's takeover of Kuwait, accepting the invader's argument that the territory was rightfully part of Iraq. More importantly, he vehemently opposed U.S. defense of Saudi Arabia, "possibly one of the most closed, wicked countries in the world." Franklin saw the U.S. response as an opportunity to undermine Saudi Arabia. Addressing six thousand attendees of a Calvary Chapel men's conference in Palm Springs he said, "Think about this. Much of the Middle East has been closed to the gospel for centuries. Saudi Arabia is Islam's geographic center.

"Right now there are over two hundred thousand American and Canadian service personnel stationed in the Persian Gulf. And I think we need to do all we can to use their presence to share with the people of that region the faith that our nation was built on."[268] He set about to organize letter writing to all U.S. troops and reasoned that a massive onslaught of such missives would overwhelm the ability of alleged Saudi censors to stanch the flow. At the same time he asserted that pamphlets circulated by the Saudis to help defuse an inevitable cultural clash between young Americans and a conservative Islamist society were "the equivalent of an Islamic tract to convert men and women to Islam." While he deemed such proselityzing to be wrong coming from the Mosques, he had no reservations about his own mission and instructed participants to include Christian tracts printed in Arabic with all their letters to soldiers.

Franklin's vociferous denunciation of Islam in the aftermath of 9/11 was seen by some as extreme and forgiven by many as an understandable reaction from a man who believed that Islamic fundamentalists brought down the twin towers. But Franklin routinely condemns all non-Christians, so his demonization of Muslims is, at least, consistent. In his autobiography Franklin cast an indigenous shaman as a "witch doctor" and "could sense the evil presence." In India, he confronted "hundreds of millions of people locked in the darkness of Hinduism." He experienced the "eye-opener" of "how pagan religion blinds and enslaves people."[269]

Franklin even managed to blame communism, which he equates with Satanism, for Jim Jones' legendary Christian cult. After the mass murder-and-suicide in 1978, Jonestown sat vacant for a couple of years. The taint of religious madness clung to the site, dissuading investors and redevelopers. Recognizing an opportunity, Franklin attempted to take control of the property with help from Billy's friends in Guyana. Though the deal fell through, his description of a visit there is revealing. "It had obviously been a Marxist-Leninist commune. Posters of men such as Che Guevara and other Communist leaders or heroes littered the place. Socialist slogans were written on the walls and on homemade billboards. They had obviously been there before the mass suicide."

Franklin later used Samaritan's Purse resources to provide Bibles, ministers and medical aid for the contras in Nicaragua, again battling what he described as murderous communist/satanist forces. Whenever Franklin has run into snags of any sort in his peripatetic missionary work, he has denounced all obstacles as the work of Satan.

The Southern Baptist Convention, the church Billy Graham adopted when he stepped away from his parents' Presbyterianism, shares the Grahams' enthusiasm for war. At the group's 2005 enclave, "press reports indicated that conventioneers saved their most enthusiastic applause for [Secretary of State] Condoleeza Rice who discussed the wars in Iraq and Afghanistan. The SBC was one of the few denominations whose leaders publicly supported the Iraq war. The day before Rice spoke, the denomination's resolutions committee quashed a South Carolina messenger's proposed resolution 'on the Southern Baptist Convention's support for the unjust war in Iraq.'"[270]

The SBC recognized Graham's enormous influence within its denomination at its 2006 enclave with dedication of a statue destined for its headquarters in Nashville. The seven-foot tall statue of Billy Graham is accompanied by a seventeen-foot tall cross.

Late that year, another prospective memorial to Graham—with an even taller cross—caused a dust-up between family members when Franklin announced that Billy and Ruth would be laid to rest at the new $26 million, forty thousand square foot Billy Graham Library in Charlotte. In 2005, Franklin moved BGEA headquarters from Minneapolis to Billy's birth city and the organization expects to draw two hundred thousand visitors each year to the library and grave site.

Unobligingly, Ruth said she had exacted a written agreement from Billy to be buried in The Cove, site of the Billy Graham Training Center, in Asheville. The family split on interment plans, with Billy finally announcing that he and Ruth "would decide." Ultimately, Ruth lapsed into what would be a terminal coma in June, 2007, and Billy announced that "we" have decided to be buried at the library. She was in no position to contradict him, though she had insisted on The Cove in her last public communication.

The library memorial is designed in the shape of a large barn with a four-story glass cross over the entrance and is dubbed a library, but is actually a theme park designed by former Disney techies. Just inside the door an animatronic dairy cow named "Bessie" greets people with the story of Billy's rural beginnings and urges them to follow a history trail through the barn. Think "Hall of Presidents" meets Cracker Barrel and you'll get a good picture of its rough-sawn, kitschy charm.

Franklin has said he expects that many people will hearken to the cow's message and end their visits by accepting Jesus as their personal savior. With merchandise sales which will run into the millions every year, Franklin may well be hoping that the ersatz calf will turn out to be golden—as has the rest of his father's Magic Kingdom.

Graham's crusades always tended to be white-bread affairs, and the library dedication was no exception. Of some 2000 in attendance between invited guests, the press corps, security guards, caterers, singers and ushers, no more than a bakers' dozen nonwhites were visible in the crowd, and half of those were Secret Service or entertainers. Amidst the seventy-odd people seated with board members of the Billy Graham Evangelistic Association and Franklin's Samaritan's Purse, there was one black face.

The Billy Graham Library ensconces a convenient memory. In the exhibit titled "Response to Troubled Times," vintage TV sets behind a glass storefront run scenes of different crisis situations from the past 50 years: the aforementioned difficulties in Little Rock; Robert F. Kennedy's assassination; a May Day Parade in Red Square; the Vietnam War; Anti-War demonstrators; and 9/11. The message is that Graham was the benevolent minister bestowing calm in the wake of world-shaking events.

The focus on RFK's 1968 murder instead of King's, earlier that year, is a telling choice. When Kennedy was gunned down in that Los Angeles hotel there was a clear sense that events were spiraling out of control, but it was MLK's death on a Memphis motel balcony that had fractured the nation and helped propel Kennedy to front-runner status in the Democratic presidential primary race. Graham's inexplicable, if not inexcusable, absence from the MLK funeral presents an awkward P.R. problem which the Library curators wisely elected to elide.

Laudatory though former chief executives Bush, Carter and Clinton waxed concerning the white-maned evangelist who shared the dais at the Billy Graham Library's dedication ceremony, their speeches fell far short of the multi-media encomium housed in the building behind them. After hearing Bessie recount the legend of Billy's humble birth (near but not in a manger) on his father's dairy farm the visitor moves past a wide screen peopled by testaters whose lives have been changed by the good preacher's work. Next comes a short wait beside an antique delivery truck with "Graham Brothers' Dairy" scripted on the sides, until automatic doors glide open to admit entry to a small theater. There the visitor gets a healthy dose of crusade history with many meetings of prime ministers, potentates, the Queen and, of course, Presidents, lots of Presidents.

On then to the the the sacred chamber of the "good woman" Ruth Bell Graham, lent an air of mystery by a pagoda roof meant to summon images of her Chinese birth to missionary parents. Be assured that Billy really said those words during his speech at the dedication ceremony, "Ruth has been a good woman." His praise of his bedridden spouse would redound more comfortably if it didn't come from a man who sermonized, "As a result of sin, God cursed the woman," and other similarly accusatory references to woman's responsibility for man's fall. In the theme park, however, woman's original sin is forgiven for the nonce, and Ruth comes off as a paragon of Christian virtue, cheerfulness and a wholly worthy helpmeet to the great man.

Passing beneath a replica banner from the preacher's first successful crusade, the 1949 Los Angeles tent revival, the visitor is overwhelmed by a huge screen from which an outsized evangelist thunders warnings about the wages of sin. The visitor wishes Toto would pull back the curtain, but dogs aren't allowed in the building.

As Billy aged and his elder son rose as the obvious heir, Franklin expressed deep reluctance to take on leadership of the BGEA. At long last he was successfully enjoined to shoulder that difficult burden and moved up from the Vice Chairmanship to take the top spot in 2005. He reportedly resolved his profound reservations through fervent prayer, presumably abetted by his business school analysis of the organization's bottom line. In his autobiography, Franklin reported a similar reluctance to seize the helm of Samaritan's Purse in 1979, but finally stepped in because "income was beginning to fall off."[271]

Business lessons at Seattle Pacific College and Appalachian State University as well as his practical education in running crusades have doubtless helped him in his many managerial roles: president of Samaritan's Purse (United States); chairman of Samaritan's Purse International (United Kingdom), of Samaritan's Purse-Canada, of Samaritan's Purse-Netherlands, of World Medical Mission and of Mafraq Sanitorium (Jordan); chair of The Cove committee (which oversees the Billy Graham Training Center in Asheville); and a board member of Blue Ridge Broadcasting.

Though Franklin seems unlikely to escape the shadow of his lionized father any time soon, he has already exceeded the elder Graham's substantial income. In five years, 2000 - 2004, Billy received approximately $1.7 million in compensation from the Billy Graham Evangelistic Association. In the same period, Franklin was paid $351,000 by BGEA plus $1.3 million from Samaritan's Purse in the U.S. (the three foreign Samaritan's Purse organizations do not file U.S. tax forms). Personal tax returns are private, of course, so there is no way to accurately estimate either man's total income. These figures do not include book and periodical royalties, investments or other sources of income and neither man has been willing to provide requested personal finanical disclosure statements.

If father and son had any trouble muddling along on an annual average of $340,000 apiece in the first half of the decade, 2005 surely helped balance family budgets. Billy's compensation was just over $500,000 from BGEA, while Franklin received a little more than half that figure from BGEA alone. (2005 tax returns for Samaritan's Purse were not available as this book went to press.)

Furthermore, church financial records are not held to the same level of scrutiny as secular nonprofit or for-profit organizations. Routine IRS audits are forbidden and may only occur when ordered by upper echelon officials in the tax agency.

When Billy Graham is finally interred, his most enduring memorial is apt to be less tangible than a grandiose statue or a piety barn. He is Christianity's Big Brother, the outsize face on giant stadium screens preaching fear and promising redemption. He is the gray eminence of evangelical faith with influence far beyond the institutional boundaries of the BGEA which *Time* magazine has called "the Rolls-Royce of revival ministries."[272]

Newsweek reinforced his exalted image in its 2006 encomium, "Pilgrim's Progress," as "the man who has preached the Gospel to more human beings than anyone in history ..."[273] The magazine portrayed a contemplative man in his dotage, gentler than the terrible swift sword-wielder of days past, yet still insistent that events were moving toward Armageddon. "I've been watching the news from the Middle East," he told his interviewer. "I think that history began there, and it is going to end there. The whole Bible is centered in the Middle East ..."

According to *Newsweek*, Graham has abandoned Biblical inerrancy in favor of a less literal interpretation of what he still insists is the divine word. He thinks that the days in Genesis are merely figurative, for example, while maintaining utter certainty that Jonah was actually swallowed by a whale. Such picking and choosing has alienated some fundamentalists, but hardly diminished his reputation. He remains on good terms with those who have ridden his coattails while occasionally quibbling about narrow differences of scriptural interpretation.

Jerry Falwell, who was one of Graham's most prominent theological heirs, claimed that his ministry and Graham's were opposite, with his own pastoral mission demanding political involvement rather than evangelism. Yet Falwell, like Graham, was a member of the evangelical Southern Baptist Convention. And Graham first advocated Christian political action well before Falwell gained his own ministry 30 years ago, but Graham avoided public exposure. This is as much a measure of a larger cultural shift toward openness as anything else. If they are in some measure opposites, it might be in the selection of which foot to insert first in a tentatively opened door.

As Graham retreats from his pulpit, this nation and the world are left to grapple with his legacy. A relentless defender of the sanctity of government, he maintained that de facto segregation and violations of civil liberties were divinely ordained and thus beyond moral reproach. As the nation's most influential preacher he legitimized and abetted religious involvement in politics and advanced arguments for Christian dominion. As the messenger of corporate money men, he abetted union-bashing and displacement of indigenous tribes for monetary gain. His blandishment of capitalism has fed Milton Friedman's unfettered free trade mythology and helped unravel America's social safety net as well as its adherence to support for human rights and international law. Graham lent an ethical imprimatur to the widening gap between haves and have-nots by insisting that acceptance of Jesus was the sina qua non of faith, rather than the liberal humanistic ethos embodied in the golden rule. All the while he had the audacity to conduct his preachments for capitalism while taking a dollar here, twenty dollars there from the God-fearing poor who were most harmed by the corporate beneficiaries of his ministry.

Looking back over Graham's life and career, one must wonder what fundamentals made the man. He had a poor relationship with his father and sought approval but never measured up—Billy was the lazy son, not the worker. To the extent that the elder Graham provided a role model, it was that of a sharp trader more interested in the bottom line than personal relationships. Young Billy was known as a goody-goody tattle tale, perhaps seeking the approval of teachers to fill the parental void. A traveling crusader became his childhood idol, offering a vision of material success and societal approval, as alluring to a boy in the rural South as Hollywood stardom might be to those in other cultural milieus. Then, too, there was the hypnotic if unintelligible (to Billy) voice of Adolf Hitler, a man who swayed millions with his oratory alone. Success as a Fuller Brush salesman convinced the youngster of his own gift for gab. Next came accolades within the limited sphere of Florida Bible Institute and contact with wealthy businessmen who paid his ticket to a bigger stage. There he married well and met men with clear insight into the workings of big media, men who recognized star-power in the handsome young Graham.

An often overlooked facet of Billy Graham's character is that he was a very fearful man. Associates frequently noted his extreme agitation whenever an airplane engine changed in tone or when a flight ran into unusual weather, to the point that he set his companions on edge. His hypochondria, apparently carried over from maternal ministration in his youth, often amused his staff according to biographer William Martin when he "went running off to the Mayo Clinic at the slightest hint of illness." And it was Franklin who reported in his autobiography yet another manifestation of his father's personal insecurity— the fear that hounded Graham even when he returned home to the quiet North Carolina hamlet of Montreat where he always slept with a loaded gun at hand.

A 2007 release from the Nixon Library and Archives highlights the same aura of fearfulness, evidently communicated to Haldeman's staff. In the summer of 1972, Graham was offered a daily show on NBC-TV. An internal memo reveals the administration's advice to Graham, including, "Have you considered doing the show once a week instead of every day—it might be better for your own health."[274]

Graham's near-paranoia emerged in an interview with biographer Marshall Frady when he said, "I'll have my crucifixion. I know that. It's going to come. I'm very frightened now by the high visibility of evangelicals in the country, and there are going to arise, in my judgement, a lot of false prophets, Elmer Gantrys, to take advantage of that, and I'll be included among them—it'll be some kind of frame-up. I can already sense hostility in areas that I never sensed it before. I am hated in some areas. Why, I even have to watch what I say on the telephone now. I even have to watch what I say to my wife at home. They've got this electronic equipment now, microphones that they could aim at you from some mountaintop around here five miles away and they could pick up absolutely everything you're saying in your own bedroom. I even have to watch what I say to my wife in our own bedroom now."

Politicians have often brandished fear as well, and the twin streams of fear-based politics and fear-based religion merged to form a torrent in the popular press. Communist infiltrators, missile gaps and the domino effect each took their turn, as did the Evil Empire and, after September 11, 2001, the threat of global terrorism. Nor was the fearmongering limited to the dangers of weaponry. There was fear of gays and Catholics and blacks and welfare queens and drugs and, latterly, Arabs, anthrax, bird flu and illegal immigrants.

The twenty-first century has seen the continued rise of religion in politics, the embrace of Christianity in the United States, and Islam in other parts of the globe, as guiding principles for zealots in government. A list of nations with theocratic governments of whatever stripe is consistently synchronous with a list of governments that violate human rights. In this light, it is no coincidence that when the G.W. Bush administration sought torturers for the prisoners it kidnapped around the globe, it enlisted Afghanistan, Egypt, Morocco, Pakistan, Uzbekistan and other Islamic strongholds to connect wires to genitalia or turn the screws. Religious absolutism is as intolerant of deviation as it is tolerant of inflicting pain on the opposition. Catholic inquisitors, Uzbek boilers-in-oil, Salem witch-hunters, Saddam's Sunni prison guards and Bush's minions at Abu Ghraib or Guantanamo differ only at the level of split hairs, not in any meaningful measure of morality. The danger to our freedom from state-imposed belief systems is as real today as it was in 1750 when a gaggle of American revolutionaries formed a government shorn of divinely ordained royalty and mandated religiosity. This Constitutional separation of church and state endured for two centuries.

Today's deep religious involvement in politics in the United States is in no small part an outgrowth of Graham's work. He formed, joined or endorsed organizations that opposed civil rights, aided CIA interventions and facilitated genocide, used his political connections to circumnavigate the law and his religious network to sway electoral politics. He paved the way for Pat Robertson's death threat against Venezuelan President Hugo Chavez and his son and ministerial heir Franklin Graham's venomous oratory concerning Arabs and Islam. Franklin has been widely quoted calling Islam "a very evil and wicked religion," in the wake of 9/11. In 2006, he told the Associated Press that the Quran, "provides ample evidence that Islam encourages violence in order to win converts and to reach the ultimate goal of an Islamic world."

In every way, Graham was the spiritual father of today's right-wing religious leaders who inject themselves into the realm of politics. If he cloaked his suasion in public neutrality, it was emblematic of an era in which such intrusion was deemed unseemly. If today's practitioners are less abashed, it is in many ways reflective of the secure foundation Graham built within Republican and conservative circles.

In all of Graham's many authorized biographies, one can't miss the endless photo-ops with the rich and powerful. Graham was ever eager to shake the hands of presidents and despots, movie stars and industrial kingpins, and to offer grandiose approval of their greatness. Obsequy, more than money, seemed to drive the man—though his pockets were never empty. If he primly abjured the criminal greed of revivalists like the Bakkers, the flamboyance of Ernest Angsley or Oral Roberts and the corporeal temptations that snared Jimmy Swaggart, he was never in want. Those who travel regularly on presidential yachts and sleep at night in official mansions need not purchase their own to savor luxury.

More than any other public figure in our history, Graham undermined the Founders' skeptical deism and sought to rebrand the United States as a Christian nation, its armies the rightful instruments of Christian crusade and empire. He has lent the imprimatur of divine authority to the nation's growing militarism. Like the toxic residue left behind by the oil refiners and munitions manufacturers who were his biggest-scale contributors, the aftermath of Graham's effort is apt to bubble up in unforeseen places years after the enterprise has passed. The fruit of Billy Graham's labor is a tainted apple, and a society hungry for salvation will be a long time recovering from the ministrations of the prince of war.

Acknowledgments

This book would not have come to publication absent the active encouragement of Charlie and Laura Thomas. Charlie launched me into the project and suggested a title something like the final one. Laura offered unflagging encouragement, intellectual support and edgy humor in the clinch. You folks are great.

Researcher Matthew Hogan combed the Nixon tape archives at my behest and stumbled on other revealing documents elsewhere. Thereafter he continued to forward material far beyond the range of our initial contract simply because he believes in good scholarship. I will comfortably depend on him for future research projects and would commend him to anyone who prefers to do research in Washington, D.C. via the painless alternative of deputization.

Three interns abetted my efforts: Jasmine Ashton, Rachel Edidin and Christopher Nelson each contributed substantially to this tome. Whatever success this enterprise might achieve owes an enormous debt to their otherwise thankless labors. You folks rock!

Steve Fraser and Alex Cury both let me know at different stages that it was not a book yet. Alex steered me along until it was. Neill Andersen undertook the most careful copy-editing I have ever enjoyed or endured, and deserves my heartfelt thanks.

Carol Adams, Frank Adams, Jim Cavener, Jon Elliston, Clark Olsen, Peter Loewer and Tim Tyson all read versions of the manuscript and hurled brickbats and occasional rosebuds my way. I can't overstate my gratitude for their willingness to interrupt their lives to weigh my outpouring and offer cogent advice. You have to break eggs to make mayonaisse, and I don't mind being the egg with chefs of their caliber.

Furthermore, this work would not have been possible without the work of other biographers, particularly that of William Martin, whose authoritative work, *A Prophet With Honor*, was of constant help in framing my efforts, though he and I have reached rather different conclusions about Graham's career. Stanley Kutler's work was invaluable as well, together with his advice about possible avenues of inquiry.

However much I have been helped, aided, abetted, encouraged and led-on, errors of fact and vagaries of opinion expressed herein are mine and mine alone.

I suppose I should also acknowledge my understanding that I will find myself labeled as Satan's helper, instrument, vehicle and a whole lot more upon publication of this work. So, for the record, I don't believe in supernatural beings of any stripe and I happily acknowledge that I could be wrong. It seems to me that belief in gods has caused a whole lot more problems than it has solved.

I find myself agreeing with novelist Salman Rushdie who observed, "I do think that the question of origins and the question of ethics—which are the two big things which lead people to religion—are things which are not answered by religion. I don't believe in any of the religious stories of the origin of the universe and I don't look to priests for my moral answers."

There's the rub, exactly. People turn to religion for answers to the biggest questions and are handed meaningless homilies while being enjoined to trust and obey. And, oh yes, pass the plate. The golden rule pretty well covers the highest aspirations of human interaction and morality in my view, and that rule is decidedly secular. If we could all just do that one thing, promises of pie-in-the-sky-by-and-by would lose their appeal and origins would simply be the subject of fair-minded and ultimately unresolvable debate.

—Cecil Bothwell
October 17, 2007

Notes

1. *Time,* Feb. 7, 2005, "The 25 most influential evangelicals in America," David Van Biema,
2. *Billy Graham: A Parable of American Righteousness*, Marshall Frady, Little, Brown & Co., 1979, p.34
3. ibid., p. 35
4. ibid., p.25
5. ibid., p. 32
6. ibid., p. 31
7. ibid., p. 87
8. ibid., p. 68
9. *Just As I Am*, Billy Graham, HarperCollins Worldwide, 1997, p. 36
10. *A Parable of American Righteousness,* p. 99
11. *Just As I Am,* p. 44
12. Larry King Live, June 16 2005
13. *A Parable of American Righteousness*, p.134
14. ibid., p. 148
15. ibid., p.152
16. Asheville *Citizen-Times*, Nov. 12,1953
17. *The Media Monopoly*, 4th Edition, Ben H. Bagdikian, Beacon Press, 1992, p. 43
18. Asheville *Citizen-Times*, Nov. 8, 1953
19. *The Nation*, Sept. 25, 2006, "9/11, "An explosion out of The Towering Inferno," Tom Engelhardt
20. *To all the nations*, John Pollock, Harper & Row, Publishers, 1985, p. 39
21. *With God on Our Side: The rise of the religious right in America,* William Martin, Broadway Books, 1996, p. 29
22. *Billy Graham: Revivalist in a Secular Age,*William G. McLoughlin, Jr., Ronald Press, 1960, p.47
23. Ibid.
24. *A Prophet With Honor*, pp. 161-162
25. *Light this candle: The life and times of Alan Shephard*, Neal Thompson, Three Rivers Press, 2004, p. 207
26. *Life*, March 27, 1950
27. *The Boston Post*, April 24, 1950
28. *The Boston Daily Globe*, April 24, 1950
29. ibid.
30. *Billy Graham: God's Ambassador: A Lifelong Mission of Giving Hope to the World as witnessed by photographer Russ Busby,* W Publishing Group and the Billy Graham Evangelistic Association, 1999, p.177
31. *Just As I Am*, p. xviii
32. Billy Graham Archives, Wheaton College, photocopy of memo from

William D. Hassett, Dec. 4, 1951, from Truman Library.
33. Billy Graham Archives, Wheaton College, photocopy of memo from William D. Hassett, Dec. 24, 1951, from Truman Library .
34. *Plain Speaking*, Merle Miller, New York: Berkeley, 1973, p.363
35. *Revivalist in a Secular Age*, p. 114
36.*Vanity Fair*, August 2007, "The History Boys," David Halberstam
37. Billy Graham Archives, Wheaton College, photocopy of telegram to Truman, Dec. 28, 1951, from Truman Library
38. *A Parable of American Righteousness*, p. 237
39. *Revivalist in a secular age*, p. 145
40. *Just As I Am*, p.189
41. Ibid. p.189
42. "50 Years After Bus Boycott, MLK's Path Not Yet Taken," Ira Chernus, commondreams.org, Dec. 6, 2005
43. *The Oxford History of the American People*, p. 1072
44. *A Parable of American Righteousness*, p. 253
45. *With God on Our Side*, pp. 32-33
46 *The Nation*, July 13, 1998, "Preachers to Power," Robert Sherrill, p.12
47. *A Prophet With Honor*, p. 151
48. Asheville *Citizen-Times*, Nov. 20, 1953
49 Asheville *Citizen-Times*, Nov. 12, 1953
50. *A Parable of American Righteousness*, p. 231
51. All conversions of dollar amounts per Federal Reserve Bank calculator. http://woodrow.mpls.frb.fed.us/research/data/us/calc/
52. *A Parable of American Righteousness*, p.236
53. *American Theocracy: The peril and politics of radical religion, oil and borrowed money in the 21st century*, Kevin Phillips; Viking 2006, p. 117
54. *With God on Our Side*, pp. 33-34
55. *A Parable of American Righteousness*, p.237
56. Asheville *Citizen-Times*, Nov. 8, 1953
57. *American Theocracy*, pp. 28-29
58. From the Dwight D. Eisenhower Presidential Library A letter from Graham, Feb. 8, 1954
59. From the Dwight D. Eisenhower Presidential Library Letter from London, May 10, 1954
60. Seth Jacobs, "Sink or Swim with Ngo Dinh Diem," 81st University of Connecticut Foreign Policy Seminar, 2005
61. From the Dwight D. Eisenhower Presidential Library Letter August 24, 1956
62. *A Parable of American Righteousness*, p.238
63. ibid., p. 239
64. *Billy Graham; God's Ambassador*, p. 73
65. *The Politics of Rage*, Dan T. Carter, Simon and Schuster, 1995,p.298

66. *Revivalist in a Secular Age*, p.124
67. *Good Housekeeping*, (Oct. 1969)"Joy of Family Life," p. 103
68. *A Parable of American Righteousness*, p.44
69. *Charlotte News*, Sept. 24, 1958
70. *Just As I Am*, p. 6
71. *A Parable of American Righteousness*, p. 420
72. *A Prophet With Honor*, p. 211
73. *Thy Will be Done: The conquest of the Amazon - Nelson Rockefeller and evangelism in the age of oil*; Gerald Colby with Charlotte Dennett, HarperCollins Publishers, 1995 (all of the otherwise unattributed information about SIL, Rockefeller, etc., in this section is based on Colby's account.)
74. *Fishers of Men or Founders of Empire? The Wycliffe Bible Translators in Latin America*, David Stoll, Zed Press, London, 1982, pp. 80-81
75. ibid., p. 81
76. ibid., p. 114
77. ibid., p. 279
78. Collection 5 - T6. Interview of Vernon William Patterson by Paul Ericksen, March 5, 1985. Billy Graham Archives at Wheaton College
79. *The Preacher and the Presidents: Billy Graham in the White House*, Nancy Gibbs and Michael Duffy, Center Street, 2007, p. 61
80. *Time*, Sept. 19, 1960, "The Power of Negative Thinking"
81. *Time*, July 2, 2007, "The Catholic Conundrum," Nancy Gibbs
82. *The New York Times*, Feb. 6, 1960, "Political Criticism of Catholic Backed"
83. *The Preacher and the Presidents*, p. 94
84. Ibid, p.105
85. *A Prophet With Honor*, p. 276
86. ibid., pp. 277-278
87. From the Dwight D. Eisenhower Presidential Library, Letter from Switzerland, August 4, 1960, marked "strictly confidential"
88. *With God on Our Side*, pp. 48-49
89. *A Prophet With Honor*, p. 279
90. *Billy Graham Speaks*, Janet Lowe, John Wiley & Sons, 1999, p.149
91. *Just As I Am*, p.400
92. Asheville *Citizen-Times*, Letters, Nov. 22, 1953
93. Asheville *Citizen-Times*, Nov. 17, 1953
94. A Prophet with Honor, pp. 169-170
95. Eisenhower Presidential Library, Letter from Billy Graham to Dwight D. Eisenhower, March 27, 1956
96. *A Portrait of Billy Graham*, p. 10
97. ibid., p. 13
98. ibid., p.171
99. ibid., p.172
100. *Christian Century*, May 8, 1963
101. *With God on our Side*, p. 79

102. *Newsweek*, July 20, 197o, "The preaching and the power,"
103. *Charlotte Observer*, Aug. 15, 1965
104. ibid..
105. *The Nation*, May 29, 2006"Three Liberal Lives," Eric Alterman
106. *A Parable of American Righteousness*, p. 416
107. ibid., p
108. *Time*, April 19, 1968
109. *Pillar of Fire: America in the King Years 1963-65*, Taylor Branch;
    Simon & Schuster, 1998,p. 122
110. *The Higher Law: Thoreau on Civil Disobedience and Reform*; ed.
    Wendell Glick, with an introduction by Howard Zinn
111. *A Parable of American Righteousness*, p. 412
112. *A Prophet With Honor*, p.315
113. *Billy Graham: Evangelist to the world*, John Pollock,Harper & Row,
    Publishers, 1979, p. 168
114. *The God Delusion*, Richard Dawkins, Houghton Mifflin (2006), p. 39
115. *A Prophet With Honor*, pp. 311-312
116. Lyndon Baines Johnson Presidential Library and Museum, Letter, July 11,
1965
117. *The Nation*, July 13, 1998,"Preachers to Power," Robert Sherrill
118. *The Last Chopper: The denouement of the American role in Vietnam,
    1963-1975*, Weldon A. Brown, National University Publications,
    Kennikat Press, 1976, p. 86
119. *Pillar of Fire*, p. 595
120. *Thy Will Be Done*, p. 544
121. *A Parable of American Righteousness*, p.425
122. *Charlotte Observer* (July 25,1966)
123. Harpers, Corry
124. *Charlotte Observer*, UPI ((Nov. 15, 1969)
125. *Charlotte Observer*, AP (Dec. 30, 1968)
126. *The Progressive*, Aug. 1982,"The Conversion of Billy Graham," p. 27
127. Lyndon Baines Johnson Presidential Library and Museum
    Letter, June 21, 1968
128. *The Nation*, (May 26, 1969) "Hiring for God,"
129. *Thy Will Be Done*, p.689
130. *A Parable of American Righteousness*, p.362
131. ibid.
132. Los Angeles Press Conference, A.P. report, May 13, 1968
133. *A Parable of American Righteousness*, p. 362
134. *Thy Will Be Done*, p.689
135. ibid. pp. 690-691
136. *Inside the Company: CIA Diary*, Philip Agee, Penguin, 1975
137. *The Trial of Henry Kissinger*, Christopher Hitchens, Verso, 2002
138. Richard M. Nixon Presidential Materials, National Archive, Letter,

Sept. 20, 1969

139. Richard M. Nixon Presidential Materials, National Archive, Memorandum from H.R. Haldeman to Kissinger, Nov. 11, 1971

140. Richard M. Nixon Presidential Materials, National Archive, THE CONFIDENTIAL MISSIONARY PLAN FOR ENDING THE VIETNAM WAR, April 15, 1969.

141. http://www.crimesofwar.org/onnews/news-middleeast.html

142. *A Prophet With Honor*, p. 367

143. *International Socialist Review*, Issue 37, September–October 2004, "War Crimes and Imperial Fantasies, Noam Chomsky interviewed by David Barsamian,"

144. *A Parable of American Righteousness*, p.425

145. ibid., p. 426

146. ibid.

147. *A Prophet With Honor*, p. 360

148. Ibid.

149. *Rebel with a Cause: Finally comfortable with being Graham*, Franklin Graham, Thomas Nelson, 1997, p.59

150. *A Parable of American Righteousness*, p. 168

151. ibid., p. 69

152., *Fishers of Men or Founders of Empire?* p. 114

153. ibid., p. 115

154. *Rebel With a Cause*, p. 147

155. Montreat news conference, 1980, Tape-80, Billy Graham Archives, Wheaton College

156. *The Wars of Watergate*, Stanley I. Kutler, Alfred A. Knopf, Inc. 1990, p.72

157. *The White House Tapes: Eavesdropping on the President*, John Prados, Ed., The New Press, 2003, p. 239

158. *Evangelist to the world*, p. 108

159. *A Prophet With Honor*, p. 380

160. ibid.

161. BGEA: Crusade Activities - Collection 17 Subseries 3.1.7: Henry Holley: Honor America Day files

162. http://nixon.archives.gov/find/textual/presidential/special/staff/strachan.html

163. *A Prophet With Honor*, p.422

164. *Abuse of Power: The new Nixon Tapes*, edited and with an introduction and commentary by Stanley I. Kutler, Touchstone, 1998, p. 31

165. *A Parable of American Righteousness*, p.371

166. *The President, Richard Nixon's Secret Files*, Edited by Bruce Oudes, Harper & Row 1989, p.213

167. Nixon Library and Archives, memo from Lawrence M. Higby to H.R. Haldeman, Aug. 28, 1972, 082872_higby.pdf

168. Asheville *Citizen-Times,* March 2002
169. *The White House Tapes*, pp. 240-255
170. *The Free Press*, March 12, 2002, "When Billy Graham Planned to Kill One Million People," Alexander Cockburn
171. Nixon Library and Archives, Nixon Library and ArchivesNixon Library and ArchivesNixon Library and ArchivesLetter from Billy Graham to Richard Nixon, Feb. 4, 1972,
172. *The Haldeman Diaries: Inside the Nixon White House*, H.R. Haldeman, G.P. Putnam's Sons, 1994, p. 405
173. *The Nation*, July 13, 1998,"Preachers to Power," Robert Sherrill, p. 13
174. *Life*, Nov. 2, 1994, "The Eternal Crusader," Charles Hirschberg, p.104-108
175. *A Parable of American Righteousness*, p. 129
176. *The Haldeman Diaries*, p. 472
177. *Nixon: The triumph of a politician*, Stephen A. Ambrose, Simon and Schuster, 1989, p. 587
178. *The Haldeman Diaries*, p. 150
179. ibid. p. 481
180. *Life*, Nov. 1994, "The Eternal Crusader," Charles Hirschberg, pp. 104-108
181. Memo Nixon to Haldeman, Dec. 30, 1969, Nixon Library and Ar chives, 123069_nixon.pdf
182. Memo Haldeman to Garment, Jan. 7, 1970, Nixon Library and Archives, 011670_haldeman.pdf
183. Memorandum for The President from Henry A. Kissinger, Dec. 6 1972, Subject: Messages from Billy Graham. Nixon Archives
184. ibid
185. ibid
186. ibid
187. ibid
188. ibid
189. *A Prophet With Honor*, p. 422
190. *Billy Graham Speaks*, pp. 144-145
191. *A Prophet With Honor*, p. 423
192. From the Library of Congress, Nixon Presidential Materials Project: taped phone call from Charles Colson to Richard Nixon, Nov. 3, 1972
193. From the Library of Congress, Nixon Presidential Materials Project: A memorandum from Lawrence M. Higby to Nixon, subject: Billy Graham phone call 8:15 a.m. May 2, 1973
194. *The Nation*, July 13, 1998,"Preachers to Power," Robert Sherrill, p. 12
195. *Time*, 1990
196. *Life*, Nov. 1994, "The Eternal Crusader," Charles Hirshberg, pp. 104-108

197. *A Prophet With Honor*, p. 423
198. The sermons of Rabbi Samuel M. Stahl, "Billy Graham's Apology," April 19, 2002, Temple Beth-El, San Antonio, Texas,

http://www.beth-elsa.org/be_sermn.htm
199. *A Prophet With Honor*, p. 393
200. ibid. p. 395
201. ibid. p. 393
202. ibid. p. 423
203. ibid. p. 424
204. ibid. p. 423
205. *Charlotte Observer* (March 23, 1973)
206. *Charlotte News* (April 2, 1973)
207. *A Parable of American Righteousness*, p. 98
208. ibid., p.63
209. ibid.
210. ibid., p.128
211. *Charlotte Observer*, UPI, (March 22, 1973)
212. *The Haldeman Diaries*,p. 505
213. *Billy Graham Speaks*, p.152
214. *Graham: A Day in Billy's Life*, Gerald S. Strober, Doubleday & Company, Inc., 1976, p. 144
215. *Thy Will Be Done*, p.690
216. *The Trial of Henry Kissinger*, Christopher Hitchens, Verso, 2002
217. *The Nation*, July 13, 1998,"Preachers to Power," Robert Sherrill, p. 13
218. *American Theocracy*, p. 153
219. *Billy Graham Speaks*, p.154
220. *Inside the Oval Office: The White House Tapes from FDR to Clinton*, William Doyle, Kodansha International, 1999, p. 231
221. ibid, p. 232
222. *A Parable of American Righteousness*, p. 469
223. *American Theocracy*, p. 185
224. ibid.
225. *The Reagan Revolution*, Rowland Evans and Robert Novak, E.P. Dutton, 1981, p. 206
226. *Billy Graham: God's Ambassador*, p. 184
227. *Exit with Honor: The Life and Presidency of Ronald Reagan*, William E. Pemberton, M.E. Sharpe, Inc., 1997, p. 61
228. ibid.
229. ibid., p. 61
230. *Final Report of the Independent Counsel for Iran/Contra Matters*, Vol. I, 501
231. ibid., p. 138
232. *A Parable of American Righteousness*, p. 474

233. *Rebel With a Cause*
234. *Christianity Today*, "More than one million hear Billy Graham in England," Ron Lee, pp. 69-71
235. *The New York Times*, Oct. 17, 2004,"Without a Doubt," Ron Suskind
236. ibid.
237. *Christianity Today,* April 22, 2002,"Nixon's Ghost," editorial
238. *Christianity Today,* April 22, 2002,"Nixon's Ghost," editorial
239. All The Best: My life in letters and other writings; George H.W. Bush, Scribner, 1999, p.501
240. The Bush Presidency: First Appraisals, Colin Campbell and Bert Rockman, Chatham House Publishers, 1991, p. 98
241. American Theocracy, p. 96
242. Christian Information Bureau Bulletin, March 1991
243. People, Oct. 10, 1991,"America's Crusader," Joe Treen, p.120
244. ibid.
245. Inside the Oval Office: The White House Tapes from FDR to Clinton, p. 278
246. Christianity Today, Feb. 13, 1991,"Leaders Wrestle with Faith and War," p. 50
247. U.S. News & World Report, Nov. 19, 1990,"A revelation in the Middle East," Jeffery L. Sheler
248. The Time 100: The most important people of the century, Time
249. The Unfinished Presidency: Jimmy Carter's journey beyond the White House, Douglas Brinkley, Viking, 1998, p. 395
250. Remarks by the President on U.S.-China Relations in the 21st Century, White House Press Release, June 11, 1998
251. The Nation, July 13, 1998,"Preachers to Power," Robert Sherrill, p. 12
252. The New York Times, Oct. 5, 1997, report on videotaped message to Promise Keepers rally, by Laurie Goodstein, p.1
253. Approaching Hoofbeats: The four horsemen of the apocalypse, Billy Graham, Grason, 1983, p. 142
254. Vice: Dick Cheney and the Hijacking of the American Presidency, Lou Dubose and Jake Bernstein, Random House, 2006, p.11
255. The New Republic, May 25, 1998, "The Sanctions Sellout," Jacob Heilbrunn, p. 26 (verbatim quote atributed to National Council of Churches Associate General Secretary Albert M. Pennybacker)
256. Statement by the Rev. Billy Graham Supporting George W. Bush, CNS Information Services, Nov.6, 2000
257. Bush at War, Bob Woodward, Simon & Schuster, 2002, p. 67
258. Billy Graham's "Address at the National Prayer and Memorial Service at the Episcopal National Cathedral," Sept. 14, 2001
259. The New York Times, October 17, 2004, "Without a Doubt," Ron Suskind
260. Boston Globe,"The Bush Crusade,"James Carroll, June 28, 2005
261. The Boston Globe, June 28, 2005, "America's Crusader," James Carroll

262. Christianity Today, "Now What? A Christian response to religious terrorism," by Mark Galli, Oct. 22, 2001
263. Zbigniew Brzezinski interviewed on Charlie Rose, June 14, 2007
264. *Christianity Today*, editorial, November 12, 2001
265. *Christianity Today*, editorial, June 2003
266. *Christianity Today*, Jan. 7, 2002, "Is Islam a Religion of Peace?", Yusuf Islam, p. 37
267. *Christianity Today*, Jan. 7, 2002, "Is Islam a Religion of Peace?", Yusuf Islam, p. 37
268. *Rebel With a Cause*, p. 235
269. ibid., p. 164
270. *The New Republic*, April 21, 2003, "Franklin Graham vs. Iraq," Michelle Cottle, p. 16
271. *Rebel With a Cause*, p. 139
272. *Time*, May 13, 1996, "In the name of the father," David Van Biema, p. 71
273. *Newsweek*, August 14, 2006, "Pilgrim's Progress," Jon Meacham, p. 37
274. Talking paper for phone call to Billy Graham, Haldeman Correspondence June 1972 - August 1972, White House Special Files, Nixon Presidential Materials Project

Index

For further reading (an eclectic list)

A People's History of the United States: 1492 to Present,
Howard Zinn, (Harper Perennial Modern Classics; Later printing
edition, 2005)

Oh, I hope you've already read this one!

In brief, this history is the antidote to every standard history
book any of us were exposed to during our education. Instead of
offering our history as a series of significant actions by important
leaders, it presents our history from the perspective of the people it
happened to. From the enslavement and murder conducted by
Columbus, through the decimation of natives generally, to the slave
trade and indenture (de jure or de facto) that introduced most of our
ancestors to this continent, Zinn connects the dots you have always
known were there.

As our nation and nationalism grew, he follows the money, casts
new light on the Mexican, Civil and Spanish American wars, and fills in
the blanks in the struggle for worker's and women's rights. Race
relations are a constant theme, from the quasi-liberation of the
Emancipation Proclamation to the return of repression in the early 20th
Century, and on to the civil rights struggle of the later era. The World
Wars are discussed in depth, and you will learn that there never was the
unanimity you were once led to imagine. Draft resistance, for example,
is far from the new phenomenon I thought I witnessed during the
Vietnam war. As far back as 1863 Federal troops killed about one
thousand anti-draft rioters in New York City in one day! (Making it,
interestingly enough and by far, the largest one-day death event per
capita in that city's history before 911. But, of course, it was "our" side
that did it.)

At the same time there were thousands of organized draft
resisters in the Confederacy. Such resistance continued as long as the
draft was in use. The history of labor battles is, if anything, bloodier still
and over a much wider field. No one with any trace of literacy could be
entirely ignorant of much of the material in this book, but nowhere have
I seen the threads pulled into one whole tapestry. The myths are
debunked. The nature of the class struggle is rendered crystal clear.
(How did I miss the fact that George Washington was the richest man in
America?)

The roots of today's huge and widening gap between the rich
and the rest of us are laid bare. In an afterword added for one edition,
Zinn brings the reader up to date on the Clinton years, and offers some
thoughts on how change might be effected. This offers an energizing

204 The Prince of War

and hopeful launching pad for the reader moved to action. Few will decline.

We need to connect children with this book if we believe that the world can be a better place for anyone other than the super rich. Outstanding!

A Prophet With Honor, William Martin, (Harper Perennial, 1992)

While this book ranks as the most comprehensive take on Graham's life and career, it suffers from two shortcomings. William Martin is rather too uncritical of his subject, and, like most other Graham biographers, he depends too heavily on Graham's memory. Graham has repeatedly proven to be an unreliable source concerning his own history as I documented in the present volume. But this is the go-to book for an overview of Graham's early career.

American Theocracy: The Peril and Politics of Radical Religion, Oil, and Borrowed Money in the 21st Century, Kevin Phillips, (Penguin, 2007)

Phillips has a lot to answer for, given his early career as a neocon apologist, but he has come a long way. It can be argued, however, that his background lends some measure of credibility to his later work. It certainly suggests intellectual honesty and in this volume he ties up a lot of loose ends. The confluence of religion, oil and power isn't new, but it appears to have become an overwhelming force in world politics. We are living in very dangerous times, and Phillips comparison of our economic straits with those that felled past empires is enough to make one contemplate divestiture and emigration.

Billy Graham: A Parable of American Righteousness, Marshall Frady, (Simon & Schuster, 2006)

This ranks as the most straight-ahead biography of Billy Graham published before my own effort. While not nearly as comprehensive as William Martin's work, this is a more interestingly told tale. Originally published in 1979, it catches Graham near the height of his influence and dynamism. After publication, Graham expressed dismay that he had helped Frady with the project because the author published comments and anecdotes from Graham associates that didn't reflect particularly well on the preacher.

Billy Graham and the Rise of the Republican South, Stephen P. Miller (University of Pennsylvania Press, 2009)

This decidedly non-entertaining volume will be of value to those who like their history dissected and pinned back so that every blood vessel and nerve can be traced. Reading it was a real slog, but I labored on, looking for some new insights. Steven Miller definitely did his homework and tracked down references between layers of correspondence and in the autobiographical works of third string players that a less dogged reporter could easily have missed.

The principal factual shortcoming I found in the work was Miller's tendency (all too common among Graham's mostly fawning biographers) to take Graham's word for otherwise undocumented events and report it as fact.However, he has definitely done some serious research and is somewhat less gushingly generous to his subject than most of Graham's hagiographers.

Coming Into Being: Arifacts and Texts in the Evolution of Consciousness, William Irwin Thompson, (Palgrave Macmillan, 1998)

This is the most difficult book I had read in quite some time when I wrote the following review at the turn of the century. Hmm. It still may be. As a consequence, it is one of the most rewarding books I have encountered, and I carry the sense that I will be peeling back the layers for a long time to come. In this it reminds me of R. Buckminster Fuller's *Synergetics*: the reader is encountering a world view which challenges long unquestioned assumptions and offers a reinterpretation of intellectual and spiritual history. It is not at all surprising to discover that Thompson, like Fuller, found his wellspring in mathematics, though Bucky was the child of Transcendentalists, while this author grew up in Catholicism.

Where to begin? This volume is drawn from a series of lectures the author delivered at the Cathedral of St. John the Divine, in New York City, under the auspices of the Lindesfarne Fellowship. (Lindesfarne was formed by the author in the early 70s to bring together scientists, artists, philosophers, et. al., to explore the future of consciousness.) His discussions draw on texts and artifacts from the very ancient to the most modern, and one difficulty in my fully comprehending his meaning lies in this reader's shallow knowledge of many of the source texts. That is to say, I can follow his arguments based on the brief quotes and descriptions offered, but I do not share his deep familiarity with Babylonian or Egyptian myths, with the epic tales of Ur, the Indian Vedas, Taoism, Confucianism, or the multiple variations on Quetzalcoatl in ancient tropical America. Sometimes I felt a little at sea.

A synopsis will not do this work justice, but here is my best current shot: Archaeological evidence and ancient texts indicate that there was a universal religion in the distant past. Evidence of belief in the Great Mother has turned up on every continent. It celebrated timelessness, fecundity, the mystery of all in one. Maleness was part of Femaleness. A shift occured on both the physical and mythic levels in which the son wrested power from the mother and eventually became dominant. The shift from Matriarchy to Patriarchy is one shorthand way to describe this change. This story is evidently implicit in all of the older myths preceding the version most familiar to our culture, in which the Father's son is the lead player, the Son who has come to rule both heaven and earth.

One crucial difference between Matriarchy and Patriarchy is the shift from belief in a universal source to assertion of an individual source. Though this is my own observation, not Thompson's - one practical demonstration of this shift is that up until the advent of DNA testing, fatherhood has been essentially a judicial matter, not biological. Therefore, succession of kings, or inheritance of property or title, or assertion of divinity based on being the son of a particular father, has always been subject to dispute. Motherhood (again, up until the advent of today's science - in vitro fertilization) has always been self-evident.

The author traces two thousand year cycles of emergence and crisis in a succession of cultural and mythic traditions, but sorts out enduring threads of truth. Heisenbergian uncertainty was already well understood before the oldest records in textual form. The observer changes the observation. In mathematical terms, Thompson follows our development from the arithmetic, to the geometric, to the algebraic, now morphing into the science of chaos. And in this shift, he finds a resurgence of the most ancient. One cause does not have one effect. One effect does not have a single source. The widely described "butterfly effect," suggesting that a Monarch in Mexico can cause a monsoon in Malaysia, illustrates this point.

I can no longer assert that I am simply the offspring of two parents, I am the result of everything that happened before now.

In conclusion the author suggests that we have come to another point of bifurcation, that the forces of commercial globalization are forcing a consciousness shift to global awareness. The two roads he foresees are GATT and NAFTA versus Zen, and he believes the only way we can avoid a dark age in which authoritarianism and militarism subjugate humanity is to go within. Reminding us of Lao Tzu, he says that the unyielding is prone to failure, while flexibility is strong. "If a soldier is rigid, he won't win; If a tree is rigid, it will come to its end. Rigidity and power occupy the inferior position; Suppleness, softness, weakness and delicateness occupy the superior position." Lao Tzu reminds us that a dead body is rigid, while a baby is flexible.

Thompson fervently believes our brightest future lies between exhaling and inhaling, in the transfiguring moment when one returns to full knowledge of the Great Mother.

"Let it be, let it be, let it be, let it be. Whispered words of wisdom. Let it be." -Lennon and McCartney

god is NOT great: How religion poisons everything, Christopher Hitchens, (12 Books, 2007)

Hitchens notes in his acknowledgments that he has been working on this book all of his life, and it shows. He has gathered concise and damning evidence about all of the major world religions and their impact on human life. I find it difficult to believe that any "believer" can present convincing counter arguments to his thesis that "religion poisons everything." If you want to own just one reference book to bolster your atheism and help lead others out of the darkness of ancient myth and fraudulent faith, this is the one to buy.

Shadows of Forgotten Ancestors, Carl Sagan & Ann Druyan, (Ballantine Books, 1993)

It seems unlikely that any reader of these words can be unfamiliar with Carl Sagan's extensive body of work. He was virtually without peer as a popularizer of scientific thought in our era. His public television presence as a highbrow Mr. Wizard, will be in re-runs long into the future.

Contact, the movie version of his novel concerning a future link to other intelligences has given his thinking a pop-cultural spin. Less visible to the lay public is his brilliant scientific career, with expertise in biology and astronomy that made him a key player in NASA's Mariner, Viking and Voyager space missions—searching for evidence of life out there.

This volume is just one more piece of his puzzle, and a wonderful one. Writing with Ann Druyan, who also co-wrote the *Cosmos* television series, Sagan here explores the story of our beginnings. From life's emergence the authors trace the threads of chemistry and biology that have come together as the human species. The emphasis is everywhere on transition—the constancy of change.

Numerous chapters conclude with boxed quotes labeled "On Impermanence," eloquent reminders of that theme. We are too short-lived and too little informed of our parentage beyond a few or several generations back to be much more than orphans in a basket on the planet's doorstep, the authors posit. This is their exploration for roots.

Intriguing hints fly in from the past. Testosterone, androgen and estrogen have the same effects on birds, ants, lizards, mice and men and women. Old, old hormones, cooked up by DNA way back where all our family trees unite. Dominance and submission are the tools of social organization in chickens, komodo dragons and elk. A little xenophobia is good for genetic diversity, but too much brings failure due to incest, so the mating of occasional Romeos and Juliets is excellent for both family's gene pools. Over-specialization is every bit as hazardous as over-generalization in the game of survival. If you are too perfectly suited to your niche your kind can be wiped out by small changes -- if you are too widely adaptable you may never find a niche in which to prosper. Yin and Yang.

Shadows contains the clearest explanation I have encountered of why and how evolution works its relentless magic. (This book should be required reading for members of the Kansas School Board. Assumption of literacy on their part is just a wild guess—maybe a hireling could read it aloud at their meetings?)

A short summation will suffer from brevity, but here goes: The genetic codes which control development are incredibly long sequences composed of just four different molecular building blocks which are read-off in groups of three. It is the order of the molecules that creates the message (just as in our language where the orderly arrangement of any of 26 letters creates meaningful words.) Only a small portion of the genetic information in a cell is actually used; a lot of it is ignored (again due to parts of the message which say "read this" or "ignore this.") Mutations involve accidental re-ordering of the letters, and again, as in language, most produce nonsense words.

Mutations in "read this" sections usually result in failure of an organism but very occasionally make it more fit for survival and the improvement is passed on. Mutations in the "ignore this" sections can persist for generations without harm until a mutation in the instruction to "read this" occurs. Suddenly new possibilities are made available (rediscovery of an ancient text), again with some successful and many failing.

All of this results in what is now called "punctuated equilibrium" which suggests that evolution occurs in fits and starts, triggered most often by large scale environmental change and modification of the "read this" instruction set. Far deeper and lots wider than I can adequately describe in a brief review.

The Origin of Consciousness in the Breakdown of the Bicameral Mind, Julian Jaynes, (Mariner Books, 2000)

Jaynes' well-defended hypothesis is that the emergence of a conscious self is a recent historic development for our species, and occured about 3000 years ago—though at different times in different cultures. His evidence involves the oldest texts, and the transition from polytheism to monotheistic beliefs. He asserts that rather than struggle to find metaphoric meanings in tales of inner voices and oracles, they should be read literally. People really did hear voices of the gods, and followed those instructions: the brain hemispheres were not integrated as they are now, and non-conscious decisions in the right hemisphere were conveyed to the left and perceived as spoken language.

In those times there was no concept of "I" as we know it today, and Jaynes suggests that the birth of Judaism reflects the arrival of consciousness in the Mid-East. Tor Norretranders expanded on this idea in *The User Illusion* (Viking Penguin, 1998), and mentioned more recent research which suggests not only that Jaynes was correct, but that consciousness disappeared again somewhere between 500 and 1500 A.D.—t didn't "take" the first time and the result is known as "the dark ages."

When one considers that Greek civilization ran very smoothly for a millenium based on the intuitions of a group of women at Delphi, it is easier to be persuaded that our cherished sense of self is not a necessary pre-condition for social function. If consideration of the importance or unimportance of consciousness have piqued your interest, add this one to your reading list. It was something of a scientific blockbuster when first published in the 1980s, and it still has the power to rattle the trunks in your attic.

The Preacher and the Presidents: Billy Graham in the White House, Nancy Gibbs and Michael Duffy, (Center Street, 2007)

Given the enormous financial and investigative resources available to *Time* magazine reporters Nancy Gibbs and Michael Duffy, it shouldn't be too much to expect historical accuracy in this biography. Then again, *Time* has been an uncritical cheerleader for Graham's ministry since the day in 1950 when publisher Henry Luce visited the young minister, then a houseguest at South Carolina Governor Strom Thurmond's mansion, and decided to join William Randolph Hearst's efforts to "puff Graham." *Time* has a substantial investment in Graham's ministry, having run more than 600 stories about his career.

Unfortunately, historical accuracy isn't one of the strong points of a book that is otherwise a pleasant enough read. People make mistakes, of course, but when they tend to fall in the same direction, one begins to suspect a hidden agenda. On the other hand, simple sloppiness can't be ruled out, as when they place Graham at Bob Jones College in Greenville, S.Car., for his first year of higher education. When Graham dropped out during his freshman year that school was still located in Cleveland, Tenn.

The subtitle tells you all you need to know about the story between the covers. The book begins with Graham's rocky relationship with Harry S. Truman and ends with his fatherly embrace of George W. Bush. Those attracted to the preacher will find nothing to dislike, but also little that is new. This is the same generous tale told by Graham's publicity team in countless books, articles, movies, advertisements, TV appearances and, of course, crusades.

According to this account, from Eisenhower forward, all of the presidents have sought Graham's counsel in varying degrees, and discovered a deep well of comfort and spiritual wisdom. The authors make mild forays into Graham's political mistakes and spend a long while on his purported close friendship with and later betrayal by Nixon, but the poking is gentle and Graham emerges as an older but wiser hero.

The mistakes and omissions are telling, however. Careful to paint Nixon as the agent of darkness, they write: "The beloved Ike, Nixon charged, was `a far more complex and devious man than most people realized.'" Thus they imply that Nixon was even nasty to sweet old Dwight Eisenhower. But this can only be a deliberate misquote. In his book, *Six Crises*, Nixon actually concluded the sentence "and in the best sense of those words." His intention was to *praise* Eisenhower.

It is important for Nixon to be the sinner because the preacher the authors have chosen to present was supposedly suckered into long-term support for "Tricky Dick," and was devastated when he learned that Nixon had deceived him. Much to Graham's enduring dismay, his back-room politicking had been tape-recorded and would come back to embarrass him over and over again through ensuing years.

Nor have all of Nixon's notorious tapes yet been released.

Graham's support for civil rights is painted as enthusiastic and heartfelt, but his actual record, as noted in the present volume, is far from clear.

The Preacher and the Presidents offers comforting fiction disguised as history. It is, without doubt, a book written for believers.

The Resurgence of the Real, Charlene Spretnak, (Routledge,1999)

Spretnak's depth of insight is nearly overwhelming. In fact, the only reservation I have about recommending this book is that it is really heavy going. You're gonna have to work at it—and you may want to save Chapter 2 for later, unless the concept of "deconstructionist postmodernism" either gives you goose bumps or makes you seethe. (For what it's worth, Spretnak dispatches with the whole empty concept of d-p, but her triumphant campaign isn't for the faint of heart.)

In brief, the author's argument is that modernism—the philosophy which has ruled us for a few hundred years —has led us astray. In particular it has distorted our relationship to body, nature and place. We have accepted a separation of self (intelligence or spirit) from our physicality, of our lives from nature (as if we lived in glass boxes, or existed "on top" of it), and of our entire existence from its setting.

Modern culture embodies the pretense that it is a cloak around the planet which could as easily be draped elsewhere. Of course that is not and has never been the case, but it is the conceit of modernism that such a mental picture is the scientific or objective truth behind our subjective experience. What follows lies all around us today.

Spretnak is very optimistic that the Real is coming back with a bang, and just in time. Her philosophic defense of bioregionalism, of holistic health strategies, of Green politics, of deeply felt community, of respectful attention to ancient alternatives, and on and on, is brilliant and invigorating. As is her demolition of the underpinnings of GATT, the World Bank, modern economic theory and the use of computers in grade school classrooms, or the overweening adoption of a computerized mind-set. She blasts Sesame Street out of the water. BAM!

Most telling of all is Spretnak's explanation of why radical localism does not imply a new isolationism. She argues that we must learn to live locally in intimate contact with our bioregion, but with utter respect for the global commons. We each live in a place. We all live on earth. We must adopt solutions that work Here without deleteriously impacting There. This one may well knock your socks off. Whew.

The Structure of Scientific Revolutions, Thomas S. Kuhn, (University Of Chicago Press; 3rd edition, 1996)

It is easy to assume that everyone is familiar with Kuhn's work, but in the famously taped words of the late Richard Nixon, "That would be wrong!."

This work is a nodal point in modern understanding of how we know what we know and how science moves forward. This slim publication may be the most frequently referrenced book in my reading experience, outside of (perhaps) the Bible (which has been around somewhat longer and which makes far less sense). The gist of Kuhn's thesis is that Science pretends to progress through incremental additions to knowledge, carefully documented by hard working researchers, but it ain't so.

Kuhn carefully demonstrates that science actually lurches forward when an individual stumbles on a paradigm-shifting revelation —which most of the establishment denies vehemently until it is dragged kicking and shrieking into the new mode of thought. Though I don't own a copy, and haven't read it since a friend handed it to me in 1971 it remains vivid. I still inwardly thank Woody Boone for that gift whenever I see Kuhn mentioned.

Maybe everyone _has_ read it. If so, never mind.

The Trial of Henry Kissinger, Christopher Hitchens, (Verso, 2002)

This book is only tangentially connected to Graham, despite Graham's long association with Henry Kissinger. But if you wonder why Kissinger can't jump on a plane to just any old where these days, this is the book for you. Hitchens carefully lays out an indictment for war crimes and other misbehavior that have led more than one country to ask the wily professor to appear in court. You always knew that someone who was *that* close to Johnson, Nixon and both Bushes couldn't be a goodun, but it's much worse than you think. After reading it I am left contemplating Kissinger's Nobel Peace Prize and shaking my head.

The Triumph of Evolution ... And the Failure of Creationism, Niles Eldredge, (W.H. Freeman, 2000)

As I observed in 1999, in an essay titled "Creationism rules(?)" a large percentage of American adults—possibly 80 percent—think it is okay to teach creationism alongside evolution in public schools. Niles Eldredge is here to explain why that is misguided in the extreme. He does so authoritatively and conclusively. No one who wants quality education for our children can refute his arguments from reason.

Politics is a whole nuther ball of wax, as the author is well aware. Eldredge, a Curator in the Department of Invertebrate Paleontology at the American Museum of Natural History, is well equipped by intellect and education to pierce the propositions of the artifice known as "creation science," and inside their hollow balloon he perceives this: At root, pro-creationismists (I made that one up) believe that all morality is grounded in our being fashioned in God's image. They are certain that if we aren't divinely inspired, all Hell will break loose, for what other basis do we have for upright behavior? Therefore, it is supremely urgent to these believers that the biblical account be accepted as true—geology be damned!

This, of course, is a political argument, not science. But, in order to gain acceptance in the syllabus, apologists dress up their politics in scientific drag. While the courts usually recognize the difference when it comes to a decision (and creation science has been tossed out by judges in several states), the damage Eldredge describes is more insidious. He notes that recent editions of many elementary text books have dropped mention of evolution to avoid a fight. Teachers often teach around it. Thus the classroom battles are being lost even as the policy war is won.

Evolution represents the best scientific understanding of how we and the living world came to be. It is intrinsic to today's debates about genetically modified foods, cloning, and stem-cell research. If we want our children to become participatory citizens they need to understand the issues and the science behind them. Thus, it is *not* okay to teach myths as science, it is utterly wrong. Niles Eldredge can tell you why.

The User Illusion: Cutting Consciousness Down to Size, Tor Norretranders, (Penguin Press Science, 1999)

A very deep book, but not a difficult one, this exploration is a continuation of the journey which leads through Douglas Hofstadter's *Godel, Escher, Bach: An Eternal Golden Braid* (Vintage Books, 1979), Bucky Fuller's *Synergetics* (Macmillan, 1982) and Julian Jaynes' *The Origin of Consciousness in the Breakdown of the Bicameral Mind* (Houghton Miflin, 1982).

Norretranders launches from a discussion of thermodynamics and information theory and spins into orbit around our deepest sense of self. What is it that consciousness is conscious of?

Some surprising insights pass under the reader along the way. There is more information in a mess than in order. The expensive part of knowledge is not gaining new information but getting rid of the old. Calculation involves eliminating irrelevance -- the total on your grocery bill involves less information than all of the individual item prices taken separately, and is therefore more useful. The value of any piece of information is directly related to how much exformation (discarded data) resulted during its creation.

The brain receives about 11 million bits of information per second from sensory sources but conscious thought can handle—at most about 40 bits per second. (15-25 is more likely) There is an awful lot going on that you are completely unaware of, and which you cannot possibly ever notice. There's more, much more.

Our survival depends on unconscious decisions, in fact, consciousness lags at least .5 seconds behind events. Your brain makes decisions at least .5 seconds before "you" think "you" have made a decision. Advice to "trust your intuition" is really completely silly, you don't have a choice in that matter.

Kant was right -- any theory presupposes axioms accepted on faith, preconditions to the accepted truth. And Godel proved it -- his theorem established absolutely that no system of thought can be complete unless viewed from outside. There will never be a complete theory of everything. That truth, of course, didn't stop Kurt Godel's best buddy Albert Einstein from trying.

The *Illusion* of this work's title is drawn from the user illusion you are experiencing right now reading this review. Beginning with the Apple MacIntosh, and extending to most modern computer screens, we wired folk deal with a graphical user interface (GUI, or "gooey"). The documents on your screen, the file folders, the cascading menus, the trash can—even the words I am typing at this moment—are illusory in the sense that they do not exist inside your computer. They only exist on the screen. Inside one would find a network of impossibly complicated electrical circuits processing apparently endless strings of binary numbers.

As a computer user you don't care how the innards work, as long as they do. You interact with a surface illusion which allows you to accomplish work or play. The GUI doesn't need to be accurate or real, it needs to offer a manageable working hypothesis.

In the same way, suggests Norretranders, our consciousness is the result of one half second of processing by the most powerful computer known—the human brain. The world we interact with is entirely a simulation, a very detailed user interface, in which almost all inputs and computation are hidden. It is very deep, resulting as it does from the creation of massive exformation. (Remember that we process about 11 million bits of sensory input per second, plus whatever signals such input creates internally; and only consciously experience about 30 bits per second.) But we experience that depth as surface, just as we experience our computer "desktop" versus the quick flicker of binary code inside the CPU.

Life is largely a non-conscious experience.

Consciousness is far too slow to save us. When a car veers into your lane, you swing a ball bat, or sit on a tack, your "Me" takes over and your "I" finds out the result. The order is: input, action, consciousness.

The most troubling aspect of this unfolding of modern brain research, math, physics and information theory involves free will. It turns out that conscious free will consists of veto power. Conscious thought can halt a hand, but not un-wish to slap the silly grin off a face. This is profoundly at odds with the usual illusion that "I am in charge here." (For example: it flies in the face of the Christian notion that one can choose not to think sinful thoughts.)

Norretrander's concluding chapter is entitled, "The Sublime." Heaven is all around us, he suggests ... it exists one half second in your past. Just as a map offers the barest outline of a journey, and the computer screen a pleasantly gooey workplace, consciousness provides only a hint of the depth and richness and wonder of human experience.

Learn why good guys in Westerns usually win, why optical illusions occur, how to use a VCR and earphones to get a glimpse of preconscious processing at work and most importantly that nothing in your awareness exists sans context. "Life is really more fun when you are not conscious of it." A masterpiece.

About the author

Cecil Bothwell was elected to Asheville's City Council in 2009 following efforts by self-styled "Christians" (actually gambling interests and white supremacists) first to defeat him through a smear campaign, and then to enforce a relict phrase in the NC constitution banning office holders who "shall deny the being of Almighty God." He was subsequently named the most Courageous Elected Official of 2010 by the American Atheists. He is an investigative reporter and biographer based in Asheville, North Carolina, and has received national awards from the Association of Alternative Newsweeklies and the Society of Professional Journalists for investigative reporting, criticism and humorous commentary. He is former news editor of *Asheville City Paper*, former managing editor of Asheville's *Mountain Xpress* and founding editor of the Warren Wilson College environmental journal *Heartstone*, he served for several years as a member of the national editorial board of the Association of Alternative Newsweeklies and currently serves on the boards of two international educational nonprofit organizations working in Latin America. His weekly radio and print journal, *Duck Soup: Essays on the Submerging Culture*, remained in syndication for ten years. Today he travels across the country speaking about the nature of belief, our relationship to the natural world, and separation of church and state.　　　　　　　　　He blogs at: http://cecilbothwell.com and http:bothwellsblog.wordpress.com

CPSIA information can be obtained at www.ICGtesting.com
Printed in the USA
LVOW08s1016150713

342908LV00007B/70/P